Child Sexual Abuse

RECENT VOLUMES IN . . .
SAGE LIBRARY OF SOCIAL RESEARCH

Child Sexual Abuse

Abuse

The Initial Effects

Beverly Gomes-Schwartz
Jonathan M. Horowitz
Albert P. Cardarelli

Sage Library of Social Research 179

SAGE PUBLICATIONS
The International Professional Publishers
Newbury Park   London   New Delhi

For information address:

SAGE Publications, Inc.
2111 West Hillcrest Drive
Newbury Park, California 91320

SAGE Publications Ltd.
28 Banner Street
London EC1Y 8QE
England

SAGE Publications India Pvt. Ltd.
M-32 Market
Greater Kailash I
New Delhi 110 048 India

Printed in the United States of America

Library of Congress Cataloging-in-Publication Data

Gomes-Schwartz, Beverly.
    Child sexual abuse : the initial effects / by Beverly Gomes-Schwartz, Jonathan
M. Horowitz, Albert P. Cardarelli.
        p.   cm. — (Sage library of social research : v. 179)
    Includes bibliographical references.
    ISBN 0-8039-3610-9. — ISBN 0-8039-3611-7 (pbk.)
        1. Child molesting—United States.   I. Horowitz, Jonathan.
II. Cardarelli, Albert P.   III. Title.   IV. Series.
HQ72.U53G65   1990
362.7'6—dc20   89-24248
                                                                          CIP

FIRST PRINTING, 1990

Contents

Acknowledgments

As with any research involving issues of sensitivity and complexity, the present volume is the result of long and dedicated work by many individuals. In addition to the staff and consultants to the Family Crisis Program at Tufts New England Medical Center who were directly responsible for producing the work, a number of individuals made important contributions during various phases of the project. First, special thanks are given to Arthur Mutter, Chair, the Division of Child Psychiatry, William Monahan, Legal Counsel, both of the New England Medical Center in Boston, and Irving Hurwitz, all of whom were responsible in helping to develop and obtain funding for the project. Their advice and support throughout the study were invaluable. We also gained immeasurably from consultations with our Advisory Board members, Jeffrey Fagan, School of Criminal Justice, Rutgers University, and Arnold Rosenfeld, Executive Director of the Massachusetts Committee for Public Counsel Services. Special thanks are also extended to Pamela Swain, Director of Research and Barbara Tatem-Kelly, both from the Office of Juvenile Justice and Delinquency Prevention which supported this research.

We would also like to express appreciation to the clinical and research staff who worked with the program at its commencement: the clinicians—Virginian Eagen, Chris Holland, Eda Spielman,

Catherine Mitkus, Michael Doran, and Margaret Ward. The research assistants—Thomas Gary, Amy Grossman, Rebecca Newberry, Shari Rosenfeld, Patricia Weiss, Joan Klein, Carol Mamber, Miriam Ornstein, Roberta Calhoun, and Laura Coleman; and student aides—Cheryl Burke, Scott Cohen, and Cathleen Morrissey. These individuals made important contributions to our understanding of the clinical phenomena of child sexual abuse and to our ability to capture that information in our research data. Some of the staff moved to new endeavors before the results of the project were available and therefore could not participate directly in the writing of the final volume; we are indebted to them nevertheless. For their efforts in the editorial assistance and preparation of the Final Report submitted to the Office of Juvenile Justice and Delinquency Prevention, we would like to thank Tracy Shea, Laura Perez, and AA Medical Editors in Newton, Massachusetts.

We are also indebted to David Finkelhor of the University of New Hampshire for his contribution to the Final Report and for his advice, encouragement, and consultation, and to Patricia Bensletter, our statistical consultant, for her important contributions to the analysis of the research data.

Major thanks are also given to Kathy Rowan, Pat Mullen, Ruth Finn, and Madeleine Pidgeon of the McCormack Institute of Public Affairs at the University of Massachusetts at Boston, for their efforts in the preparation of this manuscript.

All of the above individuals, along with many others, played an important part in bringing the final report to fruition. For their efforts we are most grateful.

—Beverly Gomes-Schwartz
Jonathan Horowitz
Albert P. Cardarelli

Preface

Public awareness of child sexual abuse has changed dramatically since the research described in this book was begun by the Family Crisis Program for Sexually Abused Children at Tufts New England Medical Center in Boston. Today, child sexual victimization and incest are given widespread media coverage, while programs to educate children and parents in the prevention of child sexual abuse are being implemented around the country. Social services and psychological treatment for sexual abuse victims and their families have grown from the few pioneering programs developed during the 1970s, such as those at the Juvenile Probation Department in Santa Clara County, California, Children's Hospital National Medical Center in Washington, D.C., and Harborview Medical Center in Seattle, Washington, to a wide variety of clinical services offered through protective service agencies, mental health clinics, and justice programs throughout the country.

Despite this enormous increase in the awareness of the nature and extent of child sexual abuse, however, systematic research on the impact of sexual abuse upon children has not developed at the same pace. There is still relatively little empirical literature to guide treatment planning or decisions about the most effective legal management of sexual abuse cases at the initial stages of the abuse disclosure, and results about the long-term effects of child sexual abuse are still fragmentary and at times conflicting. In this respect, Angela Browne and David Finkelhor (1986) in their review of empirical studies of the effects of child sexual abuse conclude that it "would appear that there is no contributing factor that all studies agree on as being consistently associated with a worse prognosis" for the victims.

In an effort to establish in-depth analyses of the effects of sexual abuse on the victims and their families, the FCP for sexually abused children was established in 1980 with funding from the Office of Juvenile Justice and Delinquency Prevention. The primary objective of the program was to provide services to victims and their families, while conducting research on (1) the characteristics of sexually abused children, their families, and social environment; (2) the nature of the sexual acts these children experienced and the events that transpired following the disclosure of the abuse; and (3) the effects of the total experience upon the child and his or her family. A further objective of the program was to develop a comprehensive data base which would be useful in determining the circumstances under which children are likely to be harmed by sexual abuse, and whether psychotherapeutic intervention is capable of reducing the emotional damage associated with the abuse of the child.

The focus of this research is on the initial effects of the sexual abuse on the child and his or her family, in contrast to the long-term effects of sexual abuse as manifested in many adults (see, for example, Bagley & Ramsey, 1985, and Peters, 1984). The research also addresses some of the information needs of many practitioners who each day face questions as to whether to remove the victimized child from the home where the sexual abuse took place, whether the victim or other family members require intensive psychother-apeutic treatment to deal with the crisis, and finally, whether the intervention itself may be counterproductive to the child's best interests.

Given the importance of these questions to practitioners, a conscious decision was made to ensure that the findings were readily accessible to individuals who either regularly interact with sexual abuse cases, or make policy decisions about appropriate sexual abuse interventions. To accomplish this objective, the results are presented without detailing the fine points of statistical analyses and tests of significance throughout the text. However, for those interested in the data that underlie the findings, the statistical test results are included as appendices.

ONE

Introduction and Background to the Present Research

During the past two decades, interest in child abuse has continued to grow as society has come to recognize that the abuse of children, both physical and sexual, is a problem of significant proportion in the United States. In the 1970s, clinicians and researchers played a significant role in bringing child sexual abuse to the forefront of society at large, and to policymakers in particular. Prior to this period, much of the research focused on child abuse and neglect, and when child sexual abuse was studied, the focus was predominantly on incest rather than on the spectrum of sexual activities that are included under the rubric of child sexual abuse by today's clinicians and researchers (Tormes, 1968; Weinberg, 1955).

The notion that child abuse is a relatively new area of research is evidenced by the fact that the term *battered child* is said to have been first used by Henry Kempe in an address to the AMA in 1961 (Lynch, 1985). Since publication of Kempe's article, both researchers and clinicians have acknowledged child abuse to be a serious problem and one that includes psychological abuse, neglect, battering, sexual abuse, and exploitation. In addition to the growing interest of researchers in child abuse after Kempe's publication, policymakers also began to consider the issue when developing legislation at the state and national levels. According to Pfhol (1977), the legislatures of all 50 states passed statutes against the abuse of children by caretakers within a four-year period beginning in 1962. This "discovery" of child abuse was instrumental in the enactment of legislation making child abuse a criminal offense (Pfhol, 1977).

Given these social and legal movements, it was not long before researchers and legislators began to focus on the sexual abuse of children and adolescents as constituting a serious problem that needed to be addressed. By the late 1970s, America had discovered child sexual abuse as a social problem that required immediate attention. This discovery does not by any means indicate that child sexual abuse was nonexistent prior to this time, nor does it mean that it was of little concern to clinicians, researchers, and policy-makers. Rather, discovery refers only to the process by which behavior is raised to cultural observation, thereby allowing for a multitude of reactions by social, political, and professional groups throughout society (Finkelhor, 1979; Pfhol, 1977).

The growing concern of researchers and policymakers with child sexual abuse is witnessed by new legislation, improved reporting procedures, and the growing numbers of treatment programs throughout the United States. These changes not only provide a basis for keeping child sexual abuse in the public realm, but they also play a part in greater numbers of child sexual abuse incidents being reported to authorities. The American Humane Association, for example, has noted that while some 12,000 cases of child sexual abuse were reported to state agencies in 1977, this figure had increased to some 72,000 cases in 1983. Yet, even these figures are seen by researchers as only a fraction of the actual cases of abuse taking place each year.

The effects of child sexual abuse cannot be underestimated. The impact on the family structure as well as the psychological and emotional costs to the child are well known and documented (Browne & Finkelhor, 1986). In the following pages, some of the explanations offered for understanding the causes and effects of child sexual abuse will be briefly discussed as a basis for placing the results of the present study in an appropriate context.

UNDERSTANDING THE CAUSES OF SEXUAL ABUSE

Scientific interest in the effects of sexual abuse of children generally began with the attempt to explain the low incidence of incest. Numerous theories were developed by sociologists, anthropologists, psychologists, and psychoanalysts to explain the so-called *incest taboo* (Fox, 1980). Thus, Freud's theories concerning the origins of the incest taboo (1953), as well as those concerning childhood sexuality played a major role in shaping the attitudes and approaches of many psychologists and psychiatrists. In his early work, Freud suggested that childhood sexual trauma was indeed the cause of certain hysterical symptoms. Later, when he became interested in the role that fantasy played during childhood development, he added a footnote to his work, stating, in effect, that he had originally underemphasized the role of fantasy in reports of childhood sexual trauma. Unfortunately, many who followed Freud's approach took his comments as justification for discounting almost all reports of incest and sexual abuse presented by children.

The growing evidence showing significant numbers of children being sexually abused has raised important issues for both social scientists and clinicians as to appropriate models for explaining the causes and effects of child sexual abuse. Research aimed at understanding the causes of sexual abuse, both in terms of the clients studied, as well as the theoretical perspectives utilized to explain the results is diverse and, at times, conflicting. In terms of the theoretical models, three models have been dominant: (1) the psychiatric model, which focuses on the characteristics of the child that precipitate or increase the likelihood of sexual abuse taking place; (2) the social-psychological model, which focuses on the psychological characteristics of the offender that predispose the person to engage in sexual abuse of children; and (3) the sociological model, which addresses characteristics within the family that promote or increase the child's susceptibility to exploitation. Both intrapsychic and environmental theories have been applied to each of these broad areas. The intrapsychic approach focuses on the relationship between the psychological make-up of the participants and the occurrence of sexual abuse, while the environmental

approach emphasizes primarily an understanding of the environmental factors that impinge upon the child. Each of the three models
is briefly discussed below.

Characteristics of the Child

Some of the earliest ideas concerning the role of the child in
sexual abuse suggested an emotional complicity on the part of
the child. In attempting to explain why sexual trauma in childhood
had such a significant impact on his adult patients, Abraham (1907/
1949) suggested that often the child desired the sexual experience
(albeit unconsciously), and the sexual "abuse" was therefore seen
as a form of infantile sexual activity. This perspective was supported
by Bender and Blau (1937), who reported that the sexually abused
children they studied were unusually attractive and seductive. In
a follow-up study (Bender & Grugett, 1952) the authors again
referred to the way in which the children used their charms in
the area of sexual activity.

Although later investigators shifted from the stance of accusing
the child of seduction, the concept of children as willing participants
or collaborators continued to appear in many reports (Gagnon, 1965;
Riemer, 1940; Virkkunen, 1975; Weiss, Rogers, Darwin, & Dutton,
1955). Some research suggested that child-victims may contribute
to their own victimization by a variety of behaviors: they may
act in a way that is interpreted as suggestive by adults; they may
go along with whatever the offender suggests; they may allow
the situation to go on over time; and, they may even fail to report
the incident to anyone in authority. It has also been suggested
that a child's attempts to seek attention or nurturance may indirectly
encourage sexual advances from adults (Burton, 1968; DeFrancis,
1969). Thus, while the role of the child as seducer was de-
emphasized, many continued to imply some degree of responsibility
for bringing about the sexual abuse.

Recent authors take a different approach (e.g., Burgess, Groth,
Holmstrom, & Sgroi, 1978; Finkelhor, 1979; Hermann, 1982),
suggesting that the child's role in sexual abuse has been

overemphasized largely because of adult sexual fantasies and the attitudes inherent in a male-dominated society. Finkelhor, in his work, argues that children are not capable of true consent to sexual relations because their level of cognitive and emotional functioning is far too immature. Others attribute a child's vulnerability to sexual abuse to an inadequate environment (e.g., lack of adequate parenting figures, social isolation), rather than to specific deficits within the child (DeFrancis, 1969).

Characteristics of Sexual Offenders

A second major area of scientific inquiry concerns the personality characterization of child offenders and their relationship to sexual abuse activities. This research includes both analyses of the range of male sex offenders (Gebhard, Gagnon, Pomeroy, & Christenson, 1965; Groth & Birnbaum, 1979) and studies of the sociological and psychological characteristics of incest offenders (see Finkelhor, 1984). The primary theme emerging from this literature is that the early perception of child sexual offenders as mentally retarded, senile, or psychotic individuals (e.g., von Kraft-Ebing, 1935) is largely unaccepted today. In contrast, most such offenders demonstrate a wide range of character structures, social backgrounds, and levels of psychological functioning (Swanson, 1968). Efforts to create meaningful typologies include Groth's (1979) model of the fixated offender (one who has a persistent pattern of sexual attraction for children) and the regressed offender (one whose behavior represents a change from previous sexual behavior). Summit and Kryso's (1978) hierarchical categorization of incest offenders based on severity of character pathology presents an intriguing alternative approach.

Characteristics of the Family

Beginning in the 1960s and early 1970s, sociologists and psychologists became increasingly dissatisfied with the psychopathological model for explaining child abuse and turned increasing attention toward the relationship between family functioning and social and emotional problems (Gelles, 1973). A concomitant shift to a family perspective among clinicians working with children who had been sexually abused also occurred at this time. This perspective focused on the hypothesis that child sexual abuse most often is an outgrowth of inadequate social environment. Several authors, for example, found that child sexual abuse occurs disproportionately more often in the lowest socioeconomic strata (Benward & Densen-Gerber, 1973; DeFrancis, 1969; Finkelhor, 1979; Trainor, 1984). This association between social class and sexual abuse is seen as resulting from crowded living arrangements, illiteracy, or particular "lower class" attitudes that condone the sexual activity. Other investigators have suggested that sexual abuse of children is particularly prevalent in certain cultural subgroups because of prevailing sexual mores and attitudes (DeFrancis, 1969; Weinberg, 1955).

Several researchers have also postulated a relationship between disruptions in the family unit and subsequent sexual abuse. The absence of a stable, intact family structure is seen as a crucial variable in estimating the likelihood that a child will be sexually victimized. As poverty, poor education, and unstable family structure often coexist, it is difficult to ascertain which, if any, of these factors is more important in explaining why sexual abuse occurs. Several authors suggest that in those families where there is a history of constantly changing characters (parents separating, remarrying, or introducing new partners into the household) family ties are considerably weakened. In these families, sexual activity results because the boundaries between parent and child are less clear, and family members resort to desperate measures to sustain a sense of closeness (Henderson, 1972; Lustig, Dresser, Spellman, & Murray, 1966; Finkelhor, 1979). Alternatively, the lack of consistent parental figures may increase the likelihood that children will go unsupervised and hence be more vulnerable to all types of neglect and abuse, including sexual abuse (DeFrancis, 1969).

The notion that isolation from social influence increases the likelihood that incest taboos will be violated was initially used to explain sexual abuse in isolated rural areas. Weinberg (1955), however, found that social isolation could also occur in suburban and urban settings. Later, a number of clinicians working with victims of incest began to report composite profiles of families that were remarkably similar to Weinberg's characterizations, including passive, inadequate fathers; unsatisfactory marriages; poor sexual relations between the parents; mothers attempting to flee an unhappy situation without breaking up the family; and daughters prematurely assuming a mothering role in the family (Alexander, 1985; Meiselman, 1978). Weinberg labeled these families *endogamous*, and this concept has continued to be a theoretical underpinning for many treatment approaches (Giaretto, 1976; Rosenfeld, 1979).

ASSESSING THE EFFECTS OF ABUSE

The diversity of theories concerning the etiology of child sexual abuse is reflected in the wide range of opinions concerning its consequences and/or effects. Some studies have found that sexually abusive experiences carry no significant negative impact for the child (Bender & Grugett, 1952; Landis, 1956; Yorukoglu & Kempe, 1969), the exception being those children who have been exposed to aggressive sexual assaults (Gagnon, 1965). In opposition to these views, numerous studies have detailed significant harmful impacts of sexual abuse, particularly in incestuous relationships (Burgess & Holmstrom, 1975; Conte & Schuerman, 1987; DeFrancis, 1969; Friedrich et al., 1987; Herman & Hirschman, 1977; Kaufman, Peck, & Tagiuri, 1954; Kiser et al., 1988; McLeer et al., 1988).

Some researchers have approached the question of impact by looking at socially deviant populations for retrospective histories of sexual abuse. James and Meyerding (1977) found that a significant percentage of prostitutes had histories of being sexually abused (Lukianowicz, 1972; Silbert & Pines, 1981). Other authors (Benward & Densen-Gerber, 1973, Lloyd, 1976) have suggested that drug addicts and runaways also have frequent histories of childhood sexual abuse. High rates of childhood sexual victimization among incarcerated sexual offenders suggest that these childhood experiences may lead to sexual aggression in adulthood (Groth, 1979).

Even when there is agreement concerning the harmful impacts of child sexual abuse, clinicians often disagree about the cause of this harm. The controversy centers around the impact of social, medical, and legal agencies on the child when sexual abuse is reported. Goldstein, Freud, and Solnit, (1979), have, for example, stated, "Sexual relations between parent and child tend to remain well-guarded secrets. When suspicion is aroused, the harm done by the inquiry may be more than that caused by not intruding." Others, such as Burgess, Groth, Holmstrom, and Sgroi (1978), confirm that many adults in recalling childhood sexual abuse experiences, believe that reactions by others to the abuse were far worse than the abuse itself. It is clear then, that no single approach adequately explains why sexual abuse takes place, nor how long it affects the child, especially in regard to the long-term effects.

In addition to the varied theoretical perspectives raised to explain child sexual abuse, researchers have also directed their attention to the initial and long-term effects of abuse on the child. In following Browne and Finkelhor (1986), *initial effects* in the context of this research will refer to the reactions that take place within two years of the termination of the abuse (see also Anderson, Bach, & Griffin, 1981; Friedrich et al., 1987). In considering the long-term effects, researchers have focused on reports of adults who in seeking treatment report that they were sexually abused as children (Briere & Runtz, 1987) or they have relied on retrospective studies of adults to determine how prevalent sexual abuse is among selected populations (Finkelhor, 1979; Fromuth, 1986). The present study in restricting its case selection to those children who had been victimized within six months prior to referral, or who had first disclosed the abuse during this period, is by its nature concerned with the *initial* effects of child sexual abuse.

The following chapters discuss the Family Crisis Program (FCP) established to evaluate child sexual abuse victims, the conceptual framework used to collect data on the victims and their families, the methods used to select the treatment sample, the nature of the sexual abuse, the initial effects of the abuse on the child at the time of entry into the Family Crisis Program, the reactions of the mothers to the disclosure of the sexual abuse, and the effects of the abuse on the child and his or her family 18 months after initial entry into the program.

TWO

The Research Framework

THE FAMILY CRISIS PROGRAM

The staff of the New England Medical Center Hospital, Division of Child Psychiatry, first became interested in the problem of child sexual abuse in the late 1970s, when an increasing number of child sexual abuse victims were being seen at the hospital. Some of the children were recent victims, while others disclosed previously unreported and untreated episodes of child sexual abuse in the course of psychiatric treatment. Based on these observations, the Division of Child Psychiatry decided to develop a specialized service for sexually abused children, and in the spring of 1979, was awarded a one-year grant from the Massachusetts Department of Mental Health to implement a sexual abuse treatment team for children.

In developing these services, it readily became evident that there were limitations in the research then available about child sexual abuse. Certain subsets of sexual abuse victims and their families had been the subject of in-depth clinical study (see Meiselman, 1978 for a review of the incest literature); demographic data had been collected from broader samples of sexually abused children in various settings (e.g., following hospital contact, Tilelli, Turek, & Jaffe, 1980); and retrospective surveys of adults with childhood sexual experiences had been conducted (e.g., Finkelhor, 1979).

However, each of these lines of inquiry contributed information only on selected aspects of sexual abuse and its effects upon children. Thus, while the staff was able to draw on clinical observations about the intrapsychic functioning of incest victims (e.g., Rascovsky & Rascovsky, 1950) and perpetrators (Weiner, 1962), the dynamics of incestuous families (e.g., Kaufman, Peck, & Tagiuri, 1954), and the long-term effects that might be associated with incest (Meiselman, 1978), there was little research about psychological functioning, family interaction, and enduring effects of extrafamilial sexual abuse. In addition, although victims of sexual abuse often proceed through a variety of criminal justice, legal, and social service agencies, little systematic data had been gathered on the effects such institutions had upon abused children and their families. Without this kind of systematic information, the development of comprehensive programs for dealing with child sexual abuse is made more difficult.

The experience gained through the development of these specialized services for sexually abused children led to funding by the Office of Juvenile Justice and Delinquency Prevention to establish a research component at the Family Crisis Program (FCP). The purpose of this grant was to provide services to victims and their families, and to conduct research to examine (1) the characteristics of sexually abused children, their families, and their social environment; (2) the nature of the sexual acts these children experienced and the events that transpired following the disclosure of the abuse; and (3) the effects of the total experience upon the child and the family. A major objective of the program was to develop a comprehensive data base that would be useful in determining the circumstances under which children are likely to be harmed by sexual abuse and whether psychotherapeutic intervention can reduce the emotional damage associated with the abuse.

To meet these needs, the Family Crisis Program (FCP) was designed to synthesize some of the lines of inquiry from previous research and clinical studies in order to yield a more comprehensive description of: (1) the characteristics of the sexually abused child within the family and community; (2) the nature of sexual contacts;

(3) the events that transpire following disclosure of the abuse; and (4) the effects of the total experience upon both the child and the family. The aim of the program was to develop a data base that would be useful in determining (a) the circumstances under which children are likely to be harmed by sexual abuse, and (b) whether psychotherapeutic intervention could reduce the risk of emotional harm to such children.

ESTABLISHING A CONCEPTUAL FRAMEWORK

To conceptualize and understand the complex factors that influence whether a child is harmed by sexual abuse, the Family Crisis Program developed a framework to help guide the collection and analysis of the data on child sexual abuse. The framework focused on the complex relationships between factors in the child's development prior to the sexual abuse, the nature of the sexual contact, the manner in which the abuse was disclosed, the reactions of others, especially family members and community agencies such as protective services or the courts, and the interventions that occurred after the abuse was disclosed. Figure 2.1 depicts these relationships.

The status of the child prior to the sexual abuse represents a complex, ongoing interaction of the child's individual psychology and the input of both the family and the child's social environment. Psychodynamic theory, for example, suggests that prior to the sexual experience, the child's emotional development is strongly shaped by his or her experience with parenting figures and the broader social environment (Zetzel & Meissner, 1973). In most cases, the sexual offender may also have had a relationship with the child within the family or as a participant in the child's milieu (Finkelhor, 1979). Not only are children influenced by family and community, children also exert an impact upon both systems. Similarly, the family and community have an ongoing system of interaction. All of these systems of interaction are in place prior to the occurrence of sexual abuse. As suggested in the previous literature, all the components—the social environment, for example, a cultural

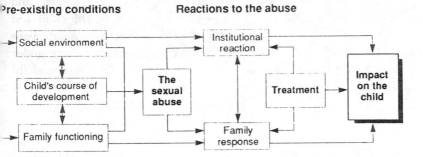

Figure 2.1. The Impact of Child Sexual Abuse: A Conceptual Framework

tolerance for, or ignoring of, sexual acting out (Gebhard et al., 1965), the course of the child's personality development, for instance, a lack of adequate nurturing (DeFrancis, 1969) and the family's dynamics, that is, an endogamic pattern of family interaction (Rosenfeld, 1979; Weinberg, 1955)—may be of significance in explaining why a particular child is victimized. Similarly, the preexisting status of the child within the family and the community is expected to influence the child's reactions to the sexual abuse.

The occurrence of sexual abuse represents a major disruption in these ongoing patterns, and the disclosure of the abuse may precipitate even greater disruption as both family members and representatives of social institutions react to the knowledge that the child has been victimized (Burgess, Groth, Holmstrom, & Sgroi, 1978; Goldstein et al., 1979). As illustrated in the proposed framework, parental and societal reactions to the abuse influence each other and are influenced by knowledge of the sexual experience and the circumstances that preceded the abuse. Representatives of institutions, such as protective services, may quickly intercede in a family because: (1) they perceive the parents as unwilling to protect the child; (2) staff anxieties are heightened by the nature of the alleged sexual episode; (3) they have previously been frustrated in working with multiple problems in the family; or (4) their previous experience with the particular child has led them to believe the child to be especially vulnerable to trauma. The strength of each factor in influencing institutional reactions varies considerably from case to case. In some instances, policemen or protective workers may act precipitously, based upon their own outrage or anxiety, without much consideration of the needs of the child or the family's capacity to respond to those needs.

Similarly, parental reactions to the abuse and its disclosure may be influenced by many factors. Parents' previous experiences with the child may contribute to a supportive, protective stance or an angry rejection of the child who has "caused" yet another problem. Institutional involvement in family life may also evoke anger, defensiveness, or blaming of the child.

Ultimately, both the institutional reactions and actions (e.g., prosecuting the offender, removing the child from the home) and the family response contribute to the impact of the sexual abuse upon the child. However, both the effect of these reactions and the abuse itself, may be mediated by treatment intervention. Clinical experience suggests that appropriate intervention can restore some of the equilibrium that was disrupted by the sexual episode and its revelation, or aid the family in restructuring pathological patterns of interaction that initially contributed to the abuse (Giaretto, 1976; Peters, 1976; Simrel, Berg, & Thomas, 1979).

Within each component of the framework (preexisting conditions, the sexual abuse, reactions to the sexual abuse, and treatment) there are likely to be several variables that either directly or indirectly influence the impact of the experience. Some of the variables hypothesized as most likely to predict impact upon the child are shown in Figure 2.2 and briefly described below.

Pre-Existing Conditions in Child's Life

Classical crisis theory suggests that the individual with a history of unsuccessful adaptation will experience greater stress and manifest greater dysfunction than an emotionally healthy counterpart in a new crisis (Aguilera & Messick, 1982; Caplan, 1964). Thus, children with histories of developmental difficulties or unresolved

Pre-Existing Conditions	The Sexual Abuse	Reactions to the Abuse	Treatment
Social Environment		*Institutional Reaction*	Family willingness to comply
Availability of resources for aiding families in distress	Duration of the abuse	Actions of protective services	Timing of treatment initiation
	Relationship with the offender	Actions of law enforcement agencies and court personnel	Modality
	Degree of violence	Medical procedures	
	Type of sexual activity		
The Child	Method for gaining the child's compliance		
	Interval between the abuse and revelation	*Family Response*	
Previous psychopathology			
History of emotional deprivation		Accusation v. support	
Level of ego development or developmental stage		Denial v. acknowledgment	
Intelligence		Ability to protect child	
Previous self-esteem		Allegiance to child versus offender	
The Family			
Psychopathology in the parents			
Ability to provide adequate nurturance			
Family disorganization			
Hostility vs. warmth toward child			

Figure 2.2. Variables Used to Predict Impact of Sexual Abuse

emotional crises may be less resilient when faced with sexual abuse, and pathological behavior patterns may intensify or new symptoms may develop. One important factor in the child's course of development, that may increase vulnerability to the stresses precipitated by sexual abuse, is a history of neglect or deprivation. The child who has consistently lacked emotional or even physical care, or who has had a history of repeated losses or separations from parental figures, may not have the psychological strengths to defend against this new disruption. Under these conditions, the child may be drawn further into an abusive situation (e.g., child prostitution) or may develop severe psychiatric symptoms.

Some children may be better able to protect themselves against the stress of sexual abuse because of their intelligence and/or high self-esteem. The intellectually capable child is better equipped to make use of therapeutic interventions that focus on exploring the child's thoughts and perceptions about the meaning of the abuse. Many children experience a distorted sense of responsibility for the sexual abuse that evokes guilt and a sense of "badness" (James, 1977; Summit & Kryso, 1978). The child who has a strong, positive self-image may be better equipped to deal with guilt or shame as opposed to the child whose self-esteem is already poor.

Although it is likely that the child's level of development bears an important relationship to the way in which the sexual abuse is understood, the nature of this relationship is complex. There is some controversy over whether younger, less cognitively mature children are more or less vulnerable to emotional trauma from sexual abuse than older children or adolescents who have a greater capacity to distinguish shades of right and wrong, and perhaps become aware of the conflicts and ambivalence in their reactions to the situation (Finkelhor, 1979; Lewis & Sarrel, 1969; MacFarlane, 1978; Meiselman, 1978; Summit & Kryso, 1978). The present study proposes that trauma may be experienced and/or expressed differently at various stages in the child's development. The very youngest children who lack a conceptual framework for under-standing the sexual activity may nonetheless experience severe diffuse anxiety that manifests itself in a variety of symptoms, such as regressions to earlier behavior (e.g., bedwetting, thumb-sucking, fearfulness, and irritability; Brant & Herzog, 1979). In contrast, adolescents experience the abuse in light of their own developing sexuality, their knowledge of social mores, and their more sophisticated expectations of the nature of human relationships.

Just as prior difficulties in the child's development may heighten vulnerability to the stresses of sexual abuse, the existence of pathology in the parents or in the functioning of the family unit may lead to behaviors that increase the risk of trauma to the child. Parents with serious emotional difficulties of their own may not be able to protect the child either before the sexual abuse occurs (Finkelhor, 1979) or after it is disclosed. Furthermore, it is likely that a family in which one or both of the parents is psychiatrically impaired will have had a history of difficulties in providing the child with sufficient emotional nurturance to insulate the child from later stresses (Newman & San Martino, 1971).

Further, difficulties in ongoing patterns of family functioning that might heighten the impact of the sexual abuse are not limited to overt psychiatric disturbances. Several authors have suggested that sexual abuse, especially incest, may occur more frequently in disorganized, socially chaotic families (DeFrancis, 1969; Finkelhor, 1979; Meiselman, 1978). It is also likely that families that include a frequently changing cast of characters and a minimal amount of structure and security for their children will be less capable of reassuring and protecting them if they are abused.

Finally, some families (those without overt psychiatric disturbance in the parents or socially disorganized life styles) may have developed negative patterns of interaction with the child that heighten the impact of the sexual abuse. For example, in some cases the child-victim may have already assumed the role of the "bad child" who causes family difficulty. In this context, the sexual abuse may be perceived as yet another instance of "getting into trouble," with the potential for the child to be subjected to angry accusations rather than the warmth and support needed to maintain psychological equilibrium.

The community and its agency representatives can also have a major impact upon the child after the sexual abuse has occurred, although the precise manner in which the pre-existing status of the child in the community contributes to the degree of trauma experienced by the child is not well documented. The ongoing availability of resources such as youth programs and physical and mental health services is a way in which the community can offer the child some support. This is especially important for children who are incest victims, as many investigators have noted the persistent psychological isolation of incest families (Meiselman, 1978; Weinberg, 1955). In these cases, most of the family's energies are turned inward with the larger world often perceived as alien and threatening (Rosenfeld, 1979). The child who is able to escape some of the psychological confinement of the incestuous family through involvement with programs outside the home (even a program such as a marching band, which does not address psychological issues) may experience some temporary reprieve from such sexual victimization, and perhaps gain enough sense of outside support to be able to disclose the secret.

The Sexual Abuse

The nature of the sexual abuse, the context in which it occurs, and the manner in which it comes to light have important implications for the way in which the child responds to the experience. In this respect, Groth (1978) has suggested that the emotional impact of the abuse is greater the closer the emotional relationship between the child and the offender; the longer the sexual activity goes on; the more physically intrusive the sexual act (e.g., penetration versus fondling versus exhibitionism); and the more aggressive the offender. Along these same lines, Finkelhor (1979) found a significant relationship between victims' retrospective reports of the trauma they had experienced and the use of physical force in the commission of the sexual act. Because Finkelhor's measure of trauma was a simple self-report obtained many years after the incident, the relationship between the previously hypothesized predictors of trauma and more comprehensive measures of the victim's functioning after the sexual abuse merits further investigation (see Bagley & Ramsey, 1986; Russell, 1986).

In addition, there are several other aspects of the sexual experience that could effect the impact upon the child, especially the amount of guilt the child experiences. MacFarlane (1978) noted that the child who feels she or he has willingly participated in the experience may be burdened with greater guilt. Building on this premise, it would be valuable to assess the manner in which the offender gained the child's compliance, as well as the child's perception of why she or he participated in the activity. The child who was coerced may be more able to attribute responsibility to the offender than the child who was bribed with either tangible or emotional inducements. Similarly, the length of time the child kept the abuse secret may relate to later feelings of guilt, as well as the assuming of responsibility for the act. Repeatedly, victims in treatment, especially adolescents or adults looking back on the experience, berate themselves for not having stopped the abuse, even when they realistically were not in a position to exert any control. Keeping the abuse secret may also reflect the child's accurate appraisal that she or he could not depend on either family or community for help and support.

In his analysis of factors related to self-reported trauma, Finkelhor (1979) found that sexual experiences with male offenders were consistently perceived as more distressing than those with female offenders, regardless of whether the child-victim was a boy or girl. His findings raise questions about the notion that contact with the same-sex offender (i.e., girls with women) is more traumatic than heterosexual contact. However, as the overwhelming majority of cases referred for treatment involve male offenders, a more important clinical question for researchers may be whether the sexual abuse of boys, which is predominantly a homosexual contact, has different effects than the abuse of girls, which is heterosexual in content (Risin & Koss, 1987).

Finkelhor's (1979) findings also challenge the assumption that age of the child is an important predictor of his or her reaction to the experience. Instead, Finkelhor found that the critical variable was the age discrepancy between the offender and victim. The greater the difference in age, the more stress the child suffered. Further investigation of the relative importance of age differences as opposed to age level or developmental stage of the child is clearly indicated (Browne & Finkelhor, 1986).

Reactions to the Sexual Abuse

The way in which a family responds to the sexual abuse of the child may be of major importance in predicting the child's ability to come to terms with the experience (Burgess, Holmstrom, & McCausland, 1978; MacFarlane, 1978). Negative reactions on the part of parents include: (1) blaming the child for the abuse; (2) refusing to believe the child's report that she or he has been sexually abused; and (3) failing to take action to protect the child from the offender. Such reactions are especially likely to occur if the family's prior functioning is pathological in character. Even in families that are usually able to provide for the child's emotional needs, the crisis engendered by the sexual abuse may temporarily impair the ability of the parents to respond sensitively and empathically.

If the abuse is intrafamilial, the potential for harmful reactions is further heightened as the family struggles with issues of divided loyalty—choosing between allying with the offender versus the victim. The child who cannot depend upon the support of a parent will be at greater risk of feeling rejected and responsible for the abuse. This child may carry a burden of self-contempt, which may be expressed through a variety of symptoms such as depression, drug or alcohol abuse, promiscuity, or other delinquent acts (Finkelhor, 1987).

Burgess, Holmstrom, and McCausland (1978) suggested that some actions that occur after the disclosure of sexual abuse may be more stressful than the sexual act itself. For example, protective service workers may remove a child from the home as the only means of protecting the child from further abuse. In other cases, however, the decision to remove the child may have more to do with a worker's anxiety in the face of the reported sexual abuse than any immediate danger to the child. If a child is removed from the home with little warning and amidst considerable tension, that child may feel responsible for disrupting the family. Self-blame added to the loss of support that family members might provide can increase the level of stress placed upon the child.

If a family decides to prosecute the offender, interventions by police and court personnel also have the potential for increasing trauma. Repeated interrogation by unfamiliar adults may frighten young children and leave them with the impression that they are the guilty parties. Overtly blaming the child or questioning the child's veracity is especially likely to occur during cross-examination by the offender's defense attorney. Although pursuing court action need not be traumatic if the child is treated with sensitivity, many factors can increase the stress upon the child and potentially increase the trauma of the entire episode (Berliner & Barbieri, 1984). Some writers suggest a number of factors that increase the stress of going to court, including dealing with unfamiliar or indifferent district attorneys and other court personnel, seeing the defendant, being exposed to public scrutiny in the court room, and waiting through long delays and postponements (Weiss & Berg, 1982; Whitcomb, 1986).

Even medical interventions aimed at protecting the child and repairing injury may inadvertently inflict trauma. Children may experience genital examination as intrusive repetitions of the sexual assault if they are not adequately prepared for the process. If such examinations are handled without acute awareness of the feelings that undressing and having their bodies carefully scrutinized might evoke in the children so recently assaulted, long-term trauma may be exacerbated (DeVine, 1980).

Treatment

The goal of therapeutic intervention with sexually abused children is to reduce the stress engendered by the sexual activity and the negative reaction to it, and to alter some of the more chronic maladaptive emotional and behavioral patterns in the child or the family. The extent to which treatment is effective in reducing trauma conceivably may be influenced by a number of variables.

The family that willingly seeks treatment is probably more likely to stay with the therapeutic program and ultimately to benefit from it. However, when sexual abuse occurs within the family there is often considerable resistance to intervention. In this regard, Giaretto (1976) has suggested that enforcing treatment compliance through legal sanctions may be the only effective means of engaging those families in which the sexual abuse is incestuous. Whether coerced treatment is more or less effective than voluntary treatment is an open question, however. Family willingness to engage in treatment may be related to the timing of the intervention. Families who reach a program shortly after the abuse has been recognized are in the midst of a crisis that challenges their habitual coping patterns. If they are not treated at this time, maladaptive responses to the abuse (e.g., denying the significance or even the occurrence of the sexual activity) may become ingrained and more difficult to alter at a later period (Briere & Runtz, 1987).

There is so little empirical literature on the assessment of treatment in cases of sexual abuse that there is little basis for predicting whether one type of intervention may be more effective than another. Some clinicians propose family approaches (Eist & Mandel, 1968); others discuss group therapy (James, 1977) or individual counseling with the child (Burgess, Holmstrom, & McClausland, 1978). In some programs (see Giaretto, 1976), a variety of treatment modalities are used. Although investigation of the relative merits of varying treatment modalities (e.g., family versus individual, crisis intervention versus long-term treatment) may yield valuable data, in this study, the FCP was only able to assess the effects of a single type of crisis-intervention treatment.

RESEARCH METHODOLOGY

To test the appropriateness of the conceptual framework described above, crisis intervention was provided to victims of sexual abuse and their families through the Family Crisis Program. The creation of this specialized clinical delivery system met two important needs. First, it ensured the delivery of treatment services for the victims; and second, it provided the opportunity to collect research data directly from the families participating in the treatment program. Developing the treatment sample from consecutive admissions to the clinic meant that appropriate subjects were readily accessible and data collection could be incorporated into the clinical evaluation process. The primary disadvantage of this procedure is that cases seen in the clinic may not necessarily represent all types of sexual abuse that occur in the population at large. It is a well-accepted fact that many cases of sexual abuse never come to the attention of persons outside the family and that a substantial proportion of those that are disclosed to outsiders never reach support systems designed specifically to investigate or treat problems associated with sexual abuse.

To obtain the most representative sample of sexual abuse cases, the FCP relied heavily on collaboration with those professionals most likely to have contact with sexually abused children. Indeed, during the course of the project, staff presented information about child sexual abuse, as well as the services offered by the FCP, to more than 100 professional groups including social service, mental health, medical, educational, and law enforcement agencies. These contacts helped generate a referral network in the catchment area served by the FCP. In addition, information regarding treatment services was presented to the public through interviews with program staff that were published in local newspapers and broadcast on radio and television. These efforts generated a substantial number of referrals from a wide spectrum of communities.

Because the treatment model was based on the premise that either the experience of being sexually abused and/or the disclosure of sexual abuse creates a crisis for the victimized child and family, it was necessary to restrict case selection to those families most likely to be experiencing a major disruption in their lives because of the occurrence or disclosure of sexual abuse. While there is disagreement as to the length of time a victim remains in crisis after a traumatic experience, only those children who had been victimized within the six months prior to referral or who had first disclosed the occurrence of ongoing sexual abuse during that same period were eligible for inclusion in the study. Although this eligibility criterion restricted some potential variability in the sample, the group of victims included in the study have a broad range of sexual experiences, ranging from a single encounter only days before referral to more than five years of ongoing victimization.

To determine whether different types of sexual abuse occurred in specific types of children or resulted in different effects on the victimized child, a broad definition of child sexual abuse was used as the guideline. In accordance with the definition of the National Center on Child Abuse and Neglect (Roth, 1978) child sexual abuse was defined as:

> contact and interactions between a child and an adult when the child is being used for the sexual stimulation of the perpetrator or another person. Sexual abuse may also be committed by a person under the age of 18 when that person is either significantly older than the victim or when the perpetrator is in a position of power or control over another.

For the purposes of this study "significantly older" meant at least a five-year age difference between the victim and perpetrator. Further, sexual abuse was defined as not including mutual sexual activity among peers. Instances involving young children who had expressed curiosity about their bodies by looking at or touching each other's genitals were not included unless one child was at least five years older than the other or had used force or coercion to get the other child to comply. Such curiosity is generally considered to be a normal phase in childhood sexual development (Martinson, 1973). Similarly, sexual stimulation or even sexual intercourse between mutually consenting adolescents was not included in the definition, even though such activity may sometimes be in violation of statutory rape laws.

Few a priori restrictions were placed on the demographic characteristics of the sample. The catchment area established for the FCP encompassed the city of Boston and those suburban communities within a 25-mile radius of the city. Children were accepted for treatment from infancy through their 18th birthday. Infants were also evaluated in the program, although research measures of the psychological functioning of children under three years old were limited by the availability of appropriate measurement tools. No restrictions were placed on sex, race, religion, or ethnic background. When more than one child in a family had been sexually victimized, each child eligible for the study was included as a research subject.

Data Collection Procedures

A variety of measures were used to collect data on the characteristics of the sexually abused child, the parents, the family environment, the social milieu, and the nature of the sexual abuse. Whenever possible, standardized self-report measures with published norms and test validation data were used so that the characteristics of the research sample could be contrasted with normative groups representing the general population or broad psychiatric populations. However, none of these standardized measures had been designed to study the issues particular to sexual abuse. Therefore, they were supplemented by questionnaires developed for other programs studying child sexual abuse (e.g., the Child and Adolescent Behavior Checklists from Children's Hospital National Medical Center, Washington, D.C.) and by an extensive series of interview questionnaires developed specifically for this study.

The data analyzed for this study fall into several broad categories. The first set of measures attempted to gauge the psychological functioning of the child at the time of entry to FCP, as well as relevant characteristics in the child's developmental history. These measures permitted the assessment of the degree of distress the child was experiencing when treatment began, as well as those background factors that may have increased the child's vulnerability to being sexually victimized or the likelihood that the child would be traumatized by the experience. Three standardized measures of the child's symptoms and emotional state were used for these analyses: (1) the Louisville Behavior Checklist; (2) the Piers-Harris Self-Concept Scale for 7- to 18-year-olds or Purdue Self-Concept

Scale for Preschool Children for 3- to 6-year-olds; and (3) Gottschalk-Gleser Content Analysis Scales.

Additional measures of the history and psychological functioning of the child's parents permitted FCP to examine the hypothesis that aspects of parents' personalities or psychological well-being are relevant in determining how a sexually abused child will respond to the abuse. The Millon Clinical Multiaxial Inventory served as a standardized measure of parent pathology, while a number of questionnaires were developed to assess aspects of the sociological environment of the sexually abused children. Finally, detailed descriptions of the sexual abuse incidents, the perpetrators, and others' reactions to the abuse were obtained with questionnaires dealing with both the victims' and the parents' report of the abuse.

When a case was referred to FCP, a research assistant was notified immediately. Unless the first appointment took place at the victim's home, the family met briefly with the research assistant to review informed consent procedures, to complete information necessary for clinic registration, and to provide data about the child's developmental history and symptoms before the first clinical appointment. During evaluation, clinicians gathered data from both the child and the parents. Additionally, two appointments were scheduled with parents and child to complete standardized self-report measures; each child was also scheduled for a psychological testing battery with a staff psychologist.

While every effort was made to obtain complete data from all families when they initially entered treatment, there were a number of constraints on data collection. Because some families withdrew from treatment after one to three sessions (21%), very limited data was collected. Moreover, the families who refused treatment were not accessible to researchers after they had left the clinic. Some individuals failed to complete specific research forms.

Other parents did not have adequate English-language skills or reading ability to complete the self-report measures. Whenever possible, the measures were administered verbally to such parents, by a research assistant with language training. Occasionally, other family members would serve as translators. However, reading questionnaires was extremely time-consuming for both research staff and clients, and often complete data could not be obtained. The traumatic nature of the problems for many families made it difficult for clinicians to collect historical data systematically. More often, the first consideration was ensuring the child's safety and attending to the immediate distress of other family members. Some facts about the history or nature of the sexual abuse simply could not be determined. In 5% to 10% of the cases, information regarding the sexual abuse was incomplete because the child was unable to report what had happened. In other cases, children who had been involved in incestuous relations with a parent for extended periods had no clear recollection of when the sexualized aspect of the relationship had commenced.

Follow-up interviews (scheduled 12-18 months after a patient had completed crisis intervention) were conducted by specially trained research assistants who followed a structured interview format. The procedure for the interviews was designed to reduce expected resistance, found among many of the treated families, to returning to the FCP clinic and reopening the issues associated with sexual abuse. Whenever possible, the interview was conducted at the victim's home, and the victimized child and each member of the family involved in the research were paid a small honorarium to compensate for their time.

The structured follow-up interview included questions to assess changes in both the child and family since they entered treatment, as well as the parents' evaluations of the sexual abuse experience and the services they received in conjunction with the abuse. To evaluate changes in emotional distress and behavioral disturbance in the child, the Louisville Child Behavior Checklist, the Piers-Harris and Purdue Self-Concept Scales, and the Child or Adolescent Behavior Checklist, developed by Children's Hospital National Medical Center (Washington, D.C.) were readministered.

The process of doing follow-up research on clinic cases once treatment has ended inevitably results in some loss of patients, and this is especially true with families of child sexual abuse victims. Often, the topic of the abuse is something families wish to avoid because the disclosure caused extreme stress and depression. Therefore, FCP fully expected that some families might take deliberate steps to make themselves inaccessible (e.g., moving without a forwarding address, obtaining an unlisted telephone number) or that they might be more likely to refuse contact with the FCP representatives. Although these expectations were to some extent confirmed, a substantial proportion of the cases in which sexual abuse of the alleged child victim had been confirmed were seen at follow-up.

The primary reasons that families were not re-interviewed resulted from their refusal to contact the FCP interviewer, and the fact that the family simply could not be found despite extensive efforts of the staff to track down changes of address or telephone number. Repeated findings that families had changed their phones to unlisted numbers suggest that these families may have wanted to avoid further contact with outside agencies.

Because many families were not interviewed for follow-up, FCP sought to determine whether there were any differences either in terms of the demographic characteristics or the nature of the sexual abuse that had occurred between those families who completed the follow-up interview and those who did not do so. This analysis indicated few differences between both groups.

Constraints on Research

Although the conceptual framework provided the basis for investigating the effects of the sexual abuse, not all of the elements could be directly translated into research data. For example, assessment of the impact of sexual abuse was complicated by the fact that sexual abuse begins to have an effect upon the child-victim as soon as it occurs, even though the child and family often do not come to clinical attention until weeks, months, or even years after the initial abuse. Thus, the psychological status of the child at the time of intake into a treatment program reflects both the child's characteristic pattern of adaptation, and the effects of the sexual experience and its disclosure.

Similarly, measurement of the factors that are hypothesized as predictors of trauma is complex. The predictors of trauma hypothesized in this research fall into the broad categories of: (1) preexisting conditions in the child's life; (2) aspects of the sexual abuse; (3) others' reactions to the abuse; and (4) treatment strategies. When the context for a research study is a treatment program, all of the categories except preexisting conditions can be measured in a relatively straightforward way during the course of the treatment intervention. In the Family Crisis Program, questionnaires were devised to record details of the sexual abuse, the steps that were taken by the family and agencies once the abuse was revealed, and aspects of the family's use of the treatment intervention.

There are a number of difficulties involved in measuring pre-existing conditions. As previously discussed, the functioning of the sexual abuse victim at the initiation of treatment is a product of both prior patterns of adaptation and responses to the abuse. Thus, it is important to note that it is virtually impossible to obtain uncontaminated measures of the child's psychological functioning prior to the abuse. While parents or an adolescent may be able to discriminate reliably between a few symptomatic behaviors that occurred before or after the sexual abuse, using such an approach to assess broader areas of functioning is unlikely to yield useful data. One way to obtain clearly differentiated pre- versus post-sexual-abuse data would be to follow a group or cohort of children hypothesized to be at greater than average risk until some of the children were abused. Such a method, however, raises questions about both the ethics of nonintervention and the economics of following large groups of children in order to study the subset that will eventually be sexually exploited.

Another more significant problem in measuring characteristics of the parents of sexually abused children did arise during this study. Assessing fathers of sexual abuse victims proved to be extremely difficult, because relatively few fathers were either available or willing to participate in treatment. This occurred in part because 55% of the children were not living with a father-figure at the time they were abused. In addition, fathers who were also the sexual abuse offenders, often were unavailable because they had left the home after the abuse was disclosed. Because research measures on fathers could only be collected for 30% of the cases in the study, interpretation of the data was inappropriate. This lack of data on fathers represents a significant limitation of the study.

The difficulties inherent in the research measurement of factors in sexual abuse place some restrictions on the degree to which the research design can address all of the issues in the proposed conceptual model. This research attempts to address as many of the major dimensions as is practical, given the limitations in the size of the sample, the amount of time staff could spend with the families, and the obvious difficulties in obtaining retrospective information.

THREE

Selection of the Treatment Sample

Coauthored with
PATRICIA SALT

Between July 1980 and January 1982, 314 children were referred
to the FCP for clinical services. This group included four distinct
subsets: (1) children who were referred for services but did not
participate in the treatment program (115 cases), (2) children who
were referred for services because they had allegedly sexually
victimized others (18 cases), (3) children for whom the allegations
of sexual abuse either could not be confirmed or were judged to
be untrue (25 cases), and (4) children who were evaluated in the
program and judged to have been sexually abused (156 cases). The
basic demographic information available for these four groups is
presented in Table 3.1, and discussion follows.

Children Referred Elsewhere or Not Treated

There has been considerable debate in the literature concerning
the proportion of sexual abuse cases that eventually reach a
treatment facility (Renvoize, 1982). Thus, the number of individuals
who indicate in surveys that they were victimized as children is

much higher than the incidence of child sexual abuse reported to authorities (DeFrancis, 1969; Finkelhor, 1979; Finkelhor & Hotaling, 1984; Gagnon, 1965; Russell, 1983; Weinberg, 1955). Although it is not possible to describe the types of cases that go unreported, limited data on cases that were referred to FCP for treatment but which did not participate in FCP intervention may give some insight into whether there are likely to be systematic factors that distinguish alleged victims who participated in treatment from those who do not.

At the FCP clinic, 39% (i.e., 115) of the total 314 clients referred as victims of child sexual abuse either were not seen at all or upon initial screening were judged to be unsuitable for the program. There were three primary reasons why these cases were not treated: (1) the FCP staff judged that the case was inappropriate for the program and referred the family elsewhere (N = 21, or 18%); (2) other arrangements were made to provide services to the family (N = 20, or 17%); or (3) the family refused services (N = 66, or 58%). A variety of reasons apply to the remaining eight families. Each of the three groups is briefly described below.

Most of the 21 cases considered inappropriate for the FCP failed to meet explicit research criteria; either the abuse had occurred or had been revealed more than six months prior to intake or the alleged victim was 18 years or older at the time of the referral. The second group of cases (N = 20, or 17%) initially appeared to be appropriate for the FCP but eventually were handled by other agencies. In seven cases the referring agency withdrew its request for services; another eight families chose to go to an agency other than the FCP for services; while the remaining five families were referred elsewhere by the FCP staff because they lived too far from the clinic to make regular appointments practical.

The majority of referrals that did not lead to treatment at the FCP (N = 66, or 58%) resulted because the family of the alleged sexual abuse victim refused to participate. Most often the refusal was explicit; 42 of these families denied that any abuse had taken place or that they needed any services. The remainder expressed an unwillingness to enter treatment by making appointments that they failed to keep or by disregarding telephone messages to contact

Table 3.1. Characteristics of All Cases Referred to the Family Crisis Program

Characteristics	Alleged Victims Treated				Alleged Victims Referred but Not Treated		Juvenile Sex Offenders	
	Confirmed		Unconfirmed					
Sex	N		N		N		N	
male	34	22%	10	40%	33	29%	18	100%
female	122	78%	15	60%	82	71%	0	0%
Race								
white	117	75%	18	72%	NA		15	83%
non-white	39	25%	7	28%	NA		3	17%
Age of child								
0-3	11	7%	5	20%	6	5%	0	0%
4-6	34	22%	7	28%	16	14%	0	0%
7-12	57	37%	7	28%	46	40%	3	17%
13-18	54	35%	6	24%	47	41%	15	83%
Religion								
Catholic	96	65%	10	40%	NA		9	50%
Protestant	34	23%	11	44%	NA		3	17%
Other	17	12%	4	16%	NA		6	33%
Socioeconomic level								
business/								
professional	20	13%	7	28%	NA		6	33%
skilled labor	29	19%	4	16%	NA		1	6%
semi-skilled	39	25%	4	16%	NA		4	22%
unskilled	68	44%	10	40%	NA		7	39%
Parent figures (at time of abuse)								
mother alone*	67	43%	15	60%	NA		5	30%
father alone	3	2%	4	16%	NA		0	0%
both parents	72	46%	5	20%	NA		8	47%
other-living arrangements	14	9%	1	4%	NA		4	23%
Totals	156		25		115		18	

*Includes 18 cases of a child's mother living with a male companion.

the clinic for appointments. These data support the widespread assumption that calculating the incidence of child sexual abuse from treated cases yields a substantial underestimation of the number of children who are victimized. If one further considers that a substantial number of cases are never referred for treatment, it becomes even more clear that treated sexual abuse cases may represent only a small minority of all cases.

Child Sexual Abuse Offenders

Although the major focus of the FCP research was to describe the experiences of child sexual abuse victims, 18 boys were referred to the program because they had sexually victimized other children. In some cases the youthful offender was referred to the FCP at the same time as the child he victimized; in other instances, FCP services were sought because there were no other specialized programs available to evaluate juvenile sex offenders. The FCP intervention with these youths consisted primarily of diagnostic evaluation. None of the offenders was seen for more than seven sessions and none of the young men continued in treatment at the FCP.

Unconfirmed Cases of Abuse

In the early stages of the project, the staff and clinicians were faced with the fact that not all allegations of sexual abuse could be confirmed. Because most cases had been handled by some other agency before being referred to the FCP, the most obvious instances of false allegations had been detected before reaching the clinic. Nevertheless, the clinical staff frequently found themselves in the position of having to determine whether adamantly denied, confused, or otherwise suspect allegations were in fact true or false. Of the 181 children evaluated, 25 cases (14%) could not be substantiated. After a thorough evaluation that typically included meetings with family members, psychological testing, and consultation with other agencies involved, the FCP determined that for 16 cases it was highly unlikely that any sexual abuse had occurred.[1] In the remaining 9 cases, clinicians at FCP were uncertain or unable to agree upon whether or not sexual abuse had occurred. A review of the clinical data revealed several reasons for a clinician's inability to determine the accuracy of an allegation; either the children were very young, or they refused to cooperate so that clinicians were unable to elicit sufficient information from either the child or the parents upon which to conclude that sexual abuse had taken place. Only those cases judged by FCP to be highly likely were included in the major analyses of sexual abuse victims (for a discussion of false allegations and their importance for research regarding child sexual abuse see Everson & Boat, 1989; Green, 1986).

The Treatment Sample

Because the major focus of this study is on victims of sexual abuse, most of the analyses deal with 156 children who met the research criteria for inclusion in the study. As discussed in Chapter 2, considerable efforts were devoted to recruiting cases of sexual abuse from as wide a geographic area and as diverse a group of referring agencies as possible. Most of these families (63%) lived in densely populated areas and described their communities as either being relatively unsafe or high crime areas. Far fewer subjects came from suburban or exurban areas where physical safety was not considered a problem. These findings do not necessarily suggest that sexual abuse is less common in more affluent communities, only that sexual abuse may be disclosed less often in more affluent families, and when such cases do occur they are more likely to be handled by private physicians or psychiatric professionals. In this respect, studies of child sexual abuse that rely upon the evaluation of identified child victims are likely to include disproportionately fewer families able to avoid any involvement with public medical or social services.

The idea that families who can avoid involvement with public social services are less likely to reach clinics is supported by the finding that the largest group of treatment cases (39%) was referred to the FCP by the Department of Social Services, the state protective service agency mandated to investigate child abuse (see Table 3.2). Referrals by school personnel such as teachers, guidance counselors, or school nurses were very rare (1%), even though the clinical staff had made numerous liaison contacts with schools. Similarly, criminal justice agencies tended to refer few patients (10% of the sample) with the majority of referrals coming from agencies designed to assist victims and witnesses in dealing with the court process, rather than the police, district attorneys, or other court officials.

Results of a survey of staff from similar agencies in the community suggest that personnel from most agencies express reluctance to appeal to agencies outside of their institutional framework for assistance in dealing with cases of child sexual abuse (Finkelhor, Gomes-Schwartz, & Horowitz, 1984). The very low rates of referral to the FCP from criminal justice and school personnel suggest that staff from these agencies may have been even less likely to make referrals than their statements of intentions in the survey would suggest.

Age and Sex of Treated Victims

Finkelhor found in his analysis of 13 studies (Finkelhor, 1979) that the average age at which children were sexually abused was between 9.3 and 10.6 years (see also Finkelhor, 1984; Russell, 1983; Wyatt, 1985). The FCP sample averaged 10.1 years of age upon entry into the clinic; 65% of the victims being under 13 (see Table 3.3). The average age at which the child was first abused was 9.1 years. These findings provide increased support for the premise that prepubertal children are the most likely victims of sexual abuse. At the time of treatment at the FCP, 58% of the girls and 79% of the boys had not yet reached puberty. Given the fact that the sexual abuse had been ongoing for years in some cases, the

Table 3.2. Sources of Referral for Confirmed Cases of
Child Sexual Abuse

Referring Source	Number of Cases	Percent
Protective services[1]	60	39%
Criminal justice	16	10%
Medical	18	11%
Mental health and social services	27	18%
School	1	1%
Self[2]	21	14%
Other	13	8%
Totals	156	101%[3]

1. Mandated state agency for reporting of child abuse.
2. Includes parents and family members of victim.
3. Due to rounding

proportion of children who were not pubertal when the abuse first started was even higher. Popular explanations presented in literature and films that child sex offenders are stimulated by the victim's budding sexuality are at odds with evidence indicating that most of the victims had not begun to exhibit secondary sex characteristics (Groth & Birnbaum, 1978).

Previous data on the ratio of female to male victims have varied with the techniques used to obtain data (Pierce & Pierce, 1985; Reinhart, 1987). In surveys of adults (Burgdorf, 1980; Finkelhor, 1979; Landis, 1956), retrospective reports of childhood sexual victimization were twice as common in females as in males. However, treatment facilities have reported ratios as high as 10 girls for every boy (DeFrancis, 1969). In this study, 78% of the victims were females, which corresponds to the results obtained from "normal" populations (Finkelhor, 1986; Risin & Koss, 1987).

Finkelhor has suggested that one reason why fewer boys are seen in clinics is that boys are more likely to be victimized at an older age, and hence are less likely to seek assistance from adults. This is consistent with the data on the age distribution of males and females seen in the FCP. In comparison with females, disproportionately more of the boy-victims were in the 4- to 6-year-old range and less were in the 13- to 18-year-old group.

Table 3.3. Age and Sex of Child Sexual Abuse Victims

Sex of Victim	Age									
	0-3 yrs		4-6 yrs		7-12 yrs		13-18 yrs		TOTALS	
	N	%	N	%	N	%	N	%	N	%
Female	9	7%	21	17%	45	37%	47	39%	122	100%
Male	2	6%	13	38%	12	35%	7	21%	34	100%

Note: $X^2(3) = 2.40$, $p < .05$

Although the FCP program treated proportionately more sexually victimized males than many other programs, there were few cases where services were sought for adolescent males unless the person had committed a sexual offense himself.

Family Socioeconomic Status

The concept that child sexual abuse is an outgrowth of an inadequate social environment has been widely discussed in studies of sexual abuse of children. Several investigators have found that victims of child sexual abuse are more likely to be found among the poorer, less educated members of the lower social classes (Benward & Densen-Gerber, 1973; DeFrancis, 1971; Finkelhor, 1979; Righton, 1981). Others have suggested that a breakdown in traditional family structures is important in explaining the etiology of sexual abuse (e.g., DeFrancis, 1969).

However, many previous efforts to study the role of social environment in explaining child sexual abuse have been subject to criticism. The primary complaint being that investigators have generalized from patient samples that were distorted by the nature of the community in which they were collected and by the strategies for obtaining cases. For example, if cases are selected from a population of incarcerated sex offenders, those with poor education and limited finances might be overrepresented. Similarly, data based upon clinic records may be distorted by the socioeconomic characteristics of the community which the clinic serves. Treatment facilities situated in white middle-class communities see few poor or black clients (see Kroth, 1979; Weiner, 1962), while those that serve an inner-city population may have high proportions of clients from minority groups and lower socioeconomic levels.

To deal with some of these problems the FCP made every effort to recruit patients from a demographically diverse set of communities, and compared the FCP clients with those of the population in the communities in which they live. By using census data from the neighborhoods within Boston and the surrounding towns from which this sample was drawn, it was possible to assess the extent to which the FCP patients deviated from the typical residents in their own communities. Although this approach does not account for differential rates of referral from communities with varying socioeconomic characteristics, it does provide a means of reducing some of the error in estimating the role of sociological factors in child sexual abuse.

In the present study, 69% of the sexually abused children came from families of lower socioeconomic status; 40% of these families derived their primary income from public assistance. The rate of public assistance is far in excess of the 10% average found in the communities in which the families resided. A comparison of the parents' educational level with averages in their communities revealed no substantial differences. Slightly fewer of the parents of sexual abuse victims were college graduates than would have been expected, but the differences were not significant. The discrepancy between educational level and dependence upon welfare suggests that the poverty in these families cannot be strictly explained by longstanding disadvantages in opportunities for education or occupational training. On the basis of the educational backgrounds of the parents, one would have expected that far fewer of the families would have been unable to provide for themselves financially. One explanation for the disproportionately high rate of welfare recipients is the prevalence of households led by single mothers living alone (i.e., 31% of the cases). Among the single-parent households in this study, 71% fell into the lowest socioeconomic group, which primarily included welfare recipients and menial service workers.

Thus, there is little evidence to suggest that the observed relationship between poverty and sexual abuse is attributable to illiteracy or particular "lower class" attitudes. Instead, the poverty in this sample seems to be strongly associated with the breakdown in traditional family patterns. Single-parent households may be more vulnerable to financial instability, and the resultant stress may play an important role in the parent-child relationships that take place.

Family Stability

In the present sample only 48, or 31%, of the children came from intact families of two natural parents, a similar percent of the children lived with the mother only (N = 49, or 31%). A substantial proportion of the children (27%) lived with a biologically unrelated parent—either a step-parent (15%) or the mother's boyfriend (12%). The remaining 17 children (11%) came from households where the father or other relative was the parent figure.

Substantial proportions of the children also came from families with other signs of family disorganization or disruption (see Table 3.4). In all, 38% of the children had been separated from their natural fathers for more than six months before the age of 6, and 17% had been separated from both parents for similar periods. The average child in the study had experienced two changes in parental figures during childhood. Among children over the age of 7, 21% experienced four or more changes in parenting. FCP clinicians judged that 78% of the children had experienced some degree of disruption of the family unit in their lifetime. It is important to note that, for some of the children, the disruptions were attributable in part to intervention by protective services. Thus, in 38% of the cases, the children had been officially identified as victims of abuse or neglect prior to the sexual abuse; 19% of the victims had been removed from their homes because of such abuse. Once a child from a disorganized family has been identified as abused, increased scrutiny of the family by the protective services agency may enhance the possibility that sexual abuse will also be uncovered.

Table 3.4. Family Environment of Child Sexual Abuse Victims

Separation from parents:	None	43%
(more than 6 months	From father	38%
before the age of 6)	From mother	3%
	From both parent	17%
		101%
Consistency of parenting	Same parents through childhood	22%
	Some disruption (e.g., divorce)	50%
	Multiple changes in parent figures	28%
		100%
Official reports of abuse	None	62%
and neglect	Once	23%
	More than once	15%
		100%
Child removed from the home	No	82%
because of prior abuse	For less than 6 months	6%
and neglect	Long-term placement	7%
	Multiple placements	6%
		101%

Note: Due to rounding off, percentages may sum to slightly more than 100.

One might wonder whether a breakdown in traditional family structure is necessarily a cause of sexual abuse. It may more often be a clue leading observers to suspect that something unusual is taking place within the family. Intact families with parents who appear to be functioning adequately in the community may be more likely to escape detection. Certainly, recent surveys of child sexual abuse among randomly selected community samples show little evidence of an association between social class and sexual victimization (Finkelhor, 1984; Peters, 1984; Russell, 1986). It is possible that the incidence of sexual abuse in more affluent families may be underestimated because such families are better able to avoid public services. Thus, it is noteworthy, and not entirely surprising, that families from the upper socioeconomic classes who were referred to the FCP tended to show more overt signs that can be interpreted as evidence of some disruption. In 35% of the referred families with business or professional status, a single parent was head of the household. In contrast, single-parent families comprise only 22% of such families in their communities. This finding supports the notion that disruptions in parenting may function both as a means of alerting outsiders to the possibility of sexual abuse, as well as a factor that increases the child's vulnerability to being abused. However, it is also important to recognize that any one indication of family disruption does not necessarily increase the risk of sexual abuse. For example, families with skilled and semiskilled occupations were not any more likely to be headed by single mothers than other households in their communities (Table 3.5). Certainly there are other ways in which a two-parent family can be disorganized. Unfortunately, census data do not permit comparison of the rates of other types of disruption, such as multiple changes in parenting among sexual abuse families and other citizens of their communities.

Race and Religion

Some investigators have suggested that sexual abuse of children is particularly prevalent in certain cultural subgroups because of prevailing sexual mores and attitudes (DeFrancis, 1969; Weinberg, 1955). Some writers (DeFrancis, 1971; Finkelhor, 1983; Lindholm, 1984) have suggested that blacks are overrepresented in reported child sexual abuse cases. Contrasts of the sexually abused children with residents of their communities on two measures of subgroups affiliation—race and religion—indicated that neither of these dimensions were related to the incidence of sexual abuse. While 75% of the children in our sample were white, the percentage in the towns from which they came was 73. In 81% of the cases the child's race was consistent with that of the majority of residents in his or her community (Russell, Schurman, & Trocki, 1988; Wyatt, 1985).

Community data on religious affiliation indicated that 68% of the residents were Catholic. This percentage is close to the 65%

Table 3.5. Incidence of Single-Parent Families by Occupation

Occupational Level of Victim's Family	Number of Families	Percent Single- Parent Families Among Sexual Abuse Victims	Percent Single- Parent Families in Respective Communities
Business-Professional	20	35%	22%
Skilled	29	21%	27%
Semi-skilled	39	28%	26%
Unskilled	68	71%	29%
Total	156		

Catholic composition in the sample. Similarly, the percent of Protestant residents (24%) in the community matches that found among the sexual abuse victims (23%).

SUMMARY

Although the research subjects who participated in the Family Crisis Program appear to be similar to those in other reports of sexual abuse, it is probably impossible to obtain a truly representative sample of all child sexual abuse cases that occur, because so much abuse remains undetected. Further, because the subjects are made up of those seeking services, the treatment sample may include fewer families who, because of their income and status, are better able to avoid detection (Weiner, 1962; Kroth, 1979).

Although the data do not provide the means to test this possibility, some support is provided for the hypothesis that poverty, when linked with family disruption, may play a role in child sexual abuse. While not all of the cases treated at the FCP involved socially disorganized families from the lowest socioeconomic backgrounds, such families were overrepresented. There are several possible ways in which poverty and disruption in the family may interact to increase the likelihood that a child will be sexually abused. Poor families, especially those led by a single parent, often lack the financial resources to sustain a stable home environment. Families may move frequently; caretakers for the children may shift, often because mothers must rely on an assortment of relatives or friends to provide intermittent help. As families become more disorganized, more people become involved in a child's life. Boundaries between adult caretaker and child become less clear, thereby making it easier for aberrant behavior to occur and to go unnoticed by other adults in the household.

Sexual abuse in such multiproblem families may be readily identified by professionals because these families are the ones who repeatedly appear on public assistance rosters and in public health clinics. The FCP experience with both child-victims and adults seeking treatment because of childhood victimization suggests that sexual abuse occurs within all social strata, but when the family presents an external image of stability and conformity to community norms, sexual abuse may be much more difficult to uncover.

Throughout this report, questions are raised concerning the ways in which untreated cases might differ from those who participated in the FCP, and how such hypothesized differences might influence the interpretation of findings. It is thought, however, that the 156 confirmed victims of sexual abuse reported in this study are representative of the types of cases most likely to come to the attention of protective service and mental health personnel in many settings.

NOTE

1. Seven of these cases involved allegations of abuse by a child against a family member and later retracted by the child. The other 9 cases were reports of abuse brought to professional attention by someone other than the child who later denied that any abuse had taken place.

FOUR

The Nature of Child Sexual Abuse: A New Look at Old Stereotypes

In the following, data on the diverse experiences that fall within the definition of child sexual abuse are presented. These experiences include a wide range of abuse, from those of a child who was shown pornographic photographs, to those in which a child was subjected to repeated sexual assaults over a period of years. The present chapter also explores some of the issues involved in the disclosure of the sexual abuse, as well as the responses of community institutions to the disclosure.

Detailed information on the nature of the sexual abuse was compiled by the clinicians who treated the child, as well as those who worked with the parents. The aim was to carefully examine what had taken place during the course of the sexual abuse, including who the offender was and what events transpired after the sexual abuse was disclosed. In most instances of confirmed abuse, both the parents' and the child's reports of the sexual abuse were strikingly congruent. Often, older children supplied clinicians with details they had not previously revealed to their parents. Conversely, much information had to be supplied by the parents of those children who, because of their age, did not possess sufficient verbal skills to describe the episode. Perhaps the most interesting cases were those where the sexualized language or behavior of a preschool youngster created some suspicion that the child had been victimized, but where neither parent nor child could provide conclusive information about any abuse that might have occurred. For example, a toddler in daycare persisted in pulling down the pants of other boys to tug at their penises. On another occasion he was found lying on top of a little girl, simulating intercourse. A 6-year-old girl raised concerns in her foster mother when she attempted to have intercourse with a younger boy living in the household. The absence of information on these cases meant that they could not be included in many of the later analyses assessing the relationship between sexual abuse and the child's emotional state.

In this chapter, the reports of both parent and child were combined to obtain the most complete description of the sexual abuse. Additional tables of statistics supporting the results described in the chapter are included in Appendix A. Overall, in only a small number of cases were details about the abuse unavailable.

CHARACTERISTICS OF THE SEXUAL ABUSE

Among the children referred to and treated at FCP, a wide variety of sexual activities were experienced. Table 4.1 shows that the overwhelming majority of the children experienced serious sexual abuse, with 28% subjected to either vaginal or anal intercourse, 38% subjected to oral genital contact or actual penetration (usually with fingers), and 23% subjected to fondling or forced to stimulate the offender manually. Attempted sexual contacts included activities in which the offender climbed into the child's bed or requested the child to touch the offender's genitals. Children who experienced intercourse tended to be older (11.4 years average) than those subjected to other forms of penetration (9.1 years average) at the time they were seen at the FCP. Perhaps the difference reflects the fact that younger children are often too small to be subjected to sexual intercourse without serious physical injury being readily observed. In this respect, no tendency was observed for offenders

Table 4.1. Sexual Abuse by Level of Severity

Type of Abuse	No.	Percent
Intercourse (vaginal or anal)	43	27.6
Oral-genital contact or object penetration	59	37.8
Fondling or mutual stimulation	36	23.1
Attempts/touching/voyeurism	10	6.4
No information	8	5.1
Totals	156	100.0

to stop short of other forms of penetration (object or digital) with younger children.

Table 4.2 shows that for 25% of the children the abuse continued for as long as one to five years before intake at FCP; with 7% being subjected to the abuse for more than five years. Few children (21%) were victims of only a single incident. These data convincingly demonstrate that unless children are able to disclose any sexual activity to which they are subjected, there is a potential for long-term abuse during their childhood. Table 4.2 also shows that the abuse may be frequent in nature as well. During the year before referral to FCP, some children had been sexually abused as much as once a week (12%), with 36% being abused from one to several times a month. Generally speaking, cases of longstanding abuse were more likely to include frequent contact, thus exacerbating the problem (see Appendix A).

For most of the children the sexual abuse was current; 43% had been abused as recently as one month before intake into FCP; 39% from one to six months before entering treatment. Longer delays between the last incident of sexual abuse and intake were more likely in cases of longstanding or frequent sexual abuse. Younger children were abused for less time and were seen sooner after their most recent experience (see Appendix A).

In terms of the total sample, two major subgroups were evident: (1) those children who had a limited amount of sexual contact shortly before referral to FCP, and (2) those children who had extended, repetitive sexual experiences that may have been

Table 4.2. Duration, Frequency, and Recency of Abuse

Duration of the Abuse	No.	Percent
Single Recent Incident	33	21
Less than Six Months	25	16
Six Months to One Year	22	14
One to Five Years	39	25
More than Five Years	11	7
Unknown/No Information	26	17
Totals	156	100%

Frequency of Abuse During Year Prior to Intake	No.	Percent
Once	50	32
Several Times	44	28
Once a Month	12	8
Weekly or More Often	19	12
None In Last Year	11	7
Unknown/No Information	20	13
Totals	156	100%

Most Recent Abuse Prior to Intake	No.	Percent
During Week Prior	19	12
During Month Prior	48	31
One to Six Months Prior	61	39
Six Months to One Year Prior	5	3
More Than One-Year Prior	12	8
Unknown/No Information	11	7
Totals	156	100%

discontinued in the period immediately before referral. Cessation of sexual activity may have occurred because the sexual abuse had been revealed and various types of agencies had already become involved with the family before referral to the FCP.

Based upon reports of both children and parents, three major strategies were used by offenders to gain the child's compliance in the sexual abuse: (1) *manipulation*, including deceiving the child, bribing the child, and resorting to offender's authority as an adult to convince the child to comply; (2) *verbal threats*; and (3) *overt aggression*, including threatening the child with a weapon or physically overpowering or beating the child (see Table 4.3). In 32% of the cases, manipulation alone was used, while in 52% manipulation was accompanied by aggression, threats, or both. The use of aggression or threats by themselves took place in only 3% of the cases. More often, the offender attempted to cajole or threaten the child verbally before violently forcing the child to perform sexual acts. The more serious forms of sexual abuse such as intercourse and penetration were more likely to involve overt aggression than were less serious forms of abuse (60% and 34% respectively). Manipulation was equally common among all acts of abuse.

In terms of injury to the child, 23% of the cases resulted in physical injuries ranging from moderate to major. For two-thirds of the children, there were no physical injuries evident at entrance to FCP. Most of the injuries consisted of relatively minor bruises or irritations. Medical examinations were completed after the sexual abuse in half of the cases but rarely added conclusive physical evidence. In only 3% of the cases did laboratory tests reveal the presence of sperm or semen; 3% showed evidence of venereal disease.

Physical injury was most serious when the offender used aggression to have sexual intercourse with the child. Girls, nonwhite children, and children from lower socioeconomic backgrounds were more likely to be injured (see Appendix A for analyses). Perhaps the most striking finding is that family members were just as likely to resort to violence as offenders who were not related to the child.

Table 4.3. Strategies Used to Gain the Child's Compliance in Sexual Activity

	No.	Percent
Manipulation only	50	32.0
Manipulation and threats	29	18.6
Manipulation and aggression	7	4.5
Manipulation, threats and aggression	44	28.2
Threats only	2	1.3
Aggression only	3	1.9
Unknown	21	13.5
Totals	156	100.0

CHARACTERISTICS OF THE OFFENDER

The majority of the children (74%) had been sexually assaulted by only one offender; a small proportion (5%), had been the victim of assaults in which several offenders had victimized the child at the same time, that is, gang rape (see Table 4.4). A total of 12% of the children were abused by several different offenders during the course of their childhood. In some of these cases, the connection between the different abusers was straightforward. For example, in one case a child was victimized by both her paternal grandfather and her father, who also had been victimized by his own father during childhood. In other instances, the factors that led to revictimization of a child were less clear. Thus, one child who had been placed in foster care because she had been sexually abused in her own home was later reabused by her foster father. It is unclear whether knowledge that a child has been involved in sexual activity affects an adult's view of that child, rendering the child more vulnerable to further sexual abuse. Alternatively, the sexually abused child may become conditioned by the experience to respond to adults in a sexualized fashion. Thus, adults with less capacity to control their impulses may construe the child's behavior as license for sexual exploitation.

In most cases (88%), the identity of the offender was reasonably certain. In the remaining instances, however, the child's inability or unwillingness to describe the abuse prevented positive identification. Information was collected on 192 offenders.[1] When there were multiple offenders, the ringleader, or initiator, in a group assault or the one responsible for the most longstanding sexual contact was identified as the primary offender. The events were then categorized by the child's relationship with the primary offender. The following discussion is based on the characteristics of the primary offender.

Almost all offenders were men (96%) who had some prior relationship with the child. Table 4.5 shows that 19% were natural parents while 22% were related. Of the total sample of offenders, 40% functioned in the role of parent. Nearly half the offenders

Table 4.4. Description of the Offenders[1]

Were there multiple offenders? (N = 156 cases)		Occupation of offender (N = 118)	
Only one	74%	Professional	4%
More than one simultaneous offender	5%	White-collar	6%
		Skilled labor	20%
More than one sequential offender	12%	Unskilled labor	25%
		Student	3%
Unknown	8%	Homemaker	1%
		Unemployed	10%
		Other	1%
Certainty of identity (N = 156 offenders)		Lived in same home as victim (N = 146)	
Unsure	11%	No	53%
Reasonably certain	17%	Yes	47%
Certain	71%		
Age (N = 142)		Did offender leave home after abuse (N = 72 who lived in home)	
18 or under	29%	No	54%
19 to 35	34%	Yes, voluntarily	14%
36 to 65	37%	Yes, under coercion	33%
Sex (N = 146)		Under influence of alcohol or drugs (N = 93)	
Male	96%	No	61%
Female	4%	Some of time during abuse	28%
		Always during abuse	11%
Race (N = 139)			
White	75%		
Black	22%		
Hispanic	4%		

1. Statistics are based on data for primary offenders. Reduction in N's reflect cases with unknown information.

lived in the same home as the victim (47%), and although 33% were nonfamily members, only 3% of all offenders were actual strangers. These figures strongly support repeated clinical observations that children usually are sexually abused by someone they know and often trust. Contrasts of FCP cases with survey data suggest that abuse by strangers may occur somewhat more

Table 4.5. Relationship of Victim with Primary Offender

Primary Offender	No.	Percent
Natural parent	30	19.2
Parental figure (not a blood relative)	32	20.5
Step-parent		(12%)
Adoptive parent		(2%)
Foster parent		(2%)
Parent's live-in partner		(5%)
Other relative	35	22.4
Uncle		(12%)
Grandfather		(3%)
Sibling		(5%)
Cousin		(3%)
Other relative		(1%)
Not a family member	51	32.7
Parent's lover		(1%)
Babysitter		(3%)
Foster sibling		(3%)
Acquaintance		(24%)
Stranger		(3%)
Other		(1%)
Unknown	8	5.1
Totals	156	99.9

Note: Due to rounding off numbers, subtotals in parentheses do not equal numbers represented in the percent column.

frequently in the general population than in children referred for services. For example, Finkelhor (1979) found that 24% of women and 30% of men recalled sexual victimizations by strangers. However, many of these experiences may not have been considered serious enough at the time they occurred to warrant clinical intervention. This observation is consistent with the fact that very few cases were referred to FCP when the most significant sexual experience was contact with an exhibitionist, even though contacts with exhibitionists constituted almost 30% of the sexual abuse experiences reported in some community surveys of adults (Russell, 1983; Wyatt, 1983).

Generally the offenders were relatively young men; half were under the age of 30, and 29% were adolescents. The demographic characteristics were quite similar to those of the victims; most being white (75%). Excluding students, who were nearly all adolescents, 82% of the adult offenders were either blue-collar workers or unemployed.

The relationship between the child and the offender had some bearing upon the type of sexual abuse that occurred. When the offender was not a family member, the abuse was shorter in duration and occurred less frequently in the year preceding intake (see Appendix A). This finding suggests that sexual assaults by acquaintances and strangers are more likely to occur as isolated instances. The physical proximity of the offender and victim that occurs when the offender is a relative or member of the child's household may play a role in allowing repeated sexual activity to go undetected.

There was some association as well between the socioeconomic background of the child's family and the child's relationship with the offender (see Table 4.6). Families at the upper end of the socioeconomic scale were most likely to seek treatment for a child who had been abused by someone outside the family. In contrast, the majority of families from semiskilled backgrounds sought treatment because the child had been abused by either a natural or a surrogate parent. These findings do not necessarily suggest that sexual abuse is more common in the lower classes, rather it is probably less likely to be reported or detected in more affluent families. Middle- and upper-middle-class families may be more willing to seek professional assistance when their child has been assaulted by an outsider than poorer families who may be less comfortable dealing with psychiatric services. The exceptionally high proportion of incest cases among the semiskilled working class is more difficult to explain. It is noteworthy however, that the proportion of cases of incest by a natural or substitute parent is essentially comparable in the lowest and the highest socioeconomic group (i.e., 36% versus 30%). Thus, there is little reason to alter our hypothesis that incest is not limited to any particular strata of society.

Table 4.6. Socioeconomic Background and Relationship Between the
Child and the Offender

		% of cases in which offender was:			
Social Class	N	Natural Parent (N = 30)	Parent Figure (N = 32)	Other Relative (N = 35)	Nonfamily Member (N = 51)
Business/ Professional	20	15%	15%	25%	45%
Skilled	29	29%	7%	21%	43%
Semiskilled	39	29%	37%	9%	26%
Unskilled	68	14%	22%	32%	32%

Overall, the study failed to find any differences in types of abuse
that could be attributed to the child's relationship with the offender.
Aggressive sexual approaches and physical injury of the child were
equally likely whether the offender was a parent, a relative, or
an acquaintance. Thus, there is little reason to believe that sexual
abuse of a child by a parent is less likely to involve physical harm.
Some children were brutally raped and beaten by fathers and
stepfathers, while others were lured into sexual activity by adult
acquaintances who relied upon the child's affection for them.

DISCLOSURE OF THE SEXUAL ABUSE

Among the cases brought to the attention of the FCP, 55% were
initially disclosed by the child (see Table 4.7). An additional 30%
of the children came to FCP because a parent, friend, or adult
in contact with the child, suspected that some form of sexual abuse
had taken place. Only 5% of the cases seen at FCP were referred
by doctors because of suspected sexual abuse. Children who told
were most likely to tell a parent or caretaker (55%), siblings (8%),
and school personnel (8%). Occasionally, abused children told adult
friends or relatives (10%). In 17% of the cases, however, the child's
initial attempt to relate the incident did not lead to help, either

Table 4.7. Disclosure of the Abuse

How was it initially revealed? (N = 156)		*Who did child tell?*	
		(N = 95 children who told)	
Child told	55%	Parent or parent-figure	55%
Parent observed sexual activity	1%	Other adult relative or friend	10%
Other person observed sexual		Sibling	8%
activity	3%	Other child	8%
Parent suspected	9%	School personnel	8%
Other person suspected	17%	Medical or mental health	
Medical evidence suggested	5%	professional	6%
Other	8%	Law enforcement official	1%
Unknown	3%	Other	2%

Length of time before child discussed abuse	
(N = 156)	
Immediately	24%
After 1 week to 1 year	21%
After more than 1 year	17%
Not at all before FCP	39%

because the child was not believed (9%) or because the responsible adult took no action (8%).

The length of time that the children kept secret the incidents of sexual abuse suggests that most children are hesitant to seek help. Only 24% told immediately after the abuse; more children told months later. Indeed, 17% waited for more than a year to disclose the abuse. Finally, 39% of the sample had not told anyone about the abuse before coming to the FCP. In analyzing the reasons why children resist reporting sexual abuse, two primary factors were indicated: (1) the fear that they would lose the affection or good will of the offender, and (2) the fear that they would be blamed for the abuse or harmed because they told.

The child's willingness to disclose the abuse was influenced by a number of characteristics of the experience, as well as the relationship of the child with the offender. Quite obviously, when a child told of the incident shortly after it had occurred, there was little opportunity for the sexual abuse to continue. These cases were also more likely to reach the FCP soon after the incident.

Both children who experienced intercourse and those who had relatively minor sexual abuse experiences, involving attempted activity or nontouching experiences such as exhibitionism, were especially likely to keep the abuse a secret (see Table 4.8). Nevertheless, a substantial portion of children who experienced attempted contacts (40%) told someone immediately. Thus, one might speculate that the reasons for not telling were quite different in these two groups. Some of the children encountering more minor sexual experiences may have failed to tell because they did not feel particularly troubled by the sexual overtures. The child who failed to reveal intercourse, on the other hand, probably did so either through fear or through a misplaced sense of responsibility for the activity. When the strategies for gaining the child's compliance had been aggressive, the child was likely either to report the incident immediately (39%) or fail to tell at all (43%). As mentioned previously, an aggressive approach occurred more often when the abuse involved intercourse.

At times a child's failure to tell about the abuse may have been linked to a sense of guilt about the abuse or concern about the offender. In instances in which the offender had manipulated the child into complying, relatively few children immediately reported the abuse (25%). Similarly, when a child was abused by a natural parent, more than 53% did not tell of the abuse. Such resistance was far more rare when the offender was a parent-figure, such as a stepfather, who had entered the child's life at a later time. Although 63% of the children in these cases waited some time before they told, relatively few continued to keep the secret (22%). These findings lead to the conclusion that children are more likely to report the abuse when they feel less loyalty toward the offender. This is supported by the observation that the immediate reporting of the abuse was most frequent when the abuser was not a member of the child's family (i.e., 39% told immediately).

These findings indicate the importance of having caretakers and clinicians facilitate the disclosure of sexual abuses. Children need to be reassured that: (1) they will not be harmed because they tell; (2) they were not responsible for the sexual approaches of an adult; and (3) the report of the abuse does not reflect disloyalty

Table 4.8. Relationship Between the Characteristics of the Sexual
Experience and Percent Who Told

	N	% who told: Immediately	Later	Never
Sex Act				
Intercourse	43	23%	23%	54%
Penetration	59	17%	50%	32%
Fondling	36	33%	44%	22%
Attempts and nontouching	10	40%	10%	50%
Strategy to Gain Child's Compliance				
Aggression present	54	39%	19%	43%
Threats	31	23%	39%	39%
Manipulation only	50	25%	42%	33%
Relationship with the Offender				
Natural parent	30	17%	30%	53%
Parent-Figure	32	16%	63%	22%
Other relative	35	17%	43%	40%
Non-family member	51	39%	28%	32%

to the abuser. Because there are many instances in which a child's
report of sexual abuse does cause difficulties for the offender, it
is equally important to assure children that they are not "bad
persons" because they disclose the abuse.

INSTITUTIONAL RESPONSES TO THE ABUSE

Once sexual abuse is disclosed, a variety of agencies may be
called upon to deal with the problem. The two main institutions
with which families interact are the state protective services agency
and the police. Protective services personnel will be called upon
to investigate if there is any possibility that the sexual activity
was perpetrated by a parent(s) or was the result of negligence
that subjected the child to increased danger of abuse. In the present
sample, protective services were involved in 64% of the cases, with
intervention more likely when the sexual abuse had been going

on for some time, and when the abuse was committed by a natural parent or a parent-figure (87%). (See Table 4.9.) More surprising is the fact that 45% of the cases of sexual abuse in which a nonfamily member was involved were also investigated by protective services. According to state law, sexual assaults not associated with parental negligence (for example, rape of an adolescent girl by boys at school) need not be reported to protective services. Thus, in this sample, many instances of abuse by acquaintances or strangers were viewed as possibly arising from inadequate protection by the child's caretakers. An alternative hypothesis is that protective service involvement for some children may have predated the sexual abuse. As noted earlier, almost 10% of the victims were living outside of their families at the time the sexual abuse occurred. In just about all these cases, protective service was involved. Similarly, protective services were involved in 89% of the cases in which the child had previously been removed from the home. In most of these cases it is possible that protective services workers had already established ongoing relationships with the families before the sexual abuse was disclosed.

In Massachusetts, the protective service agency has the legal right to remove children who have been sexually abused from their home if investigators believe the child to be in danger of further harm or abuse. In all, 22% of the children in this sample were removed from their homes as a consequence of sexual abuse (see Table 4.10). In an additional 24% of the cases, there was a shift in the child's parental figures—a parent left home or a child of divorced parents went to live with the other parent. In some of these cases, protective services had instigated the change by agreeing not to remove the child if the offender left the home. In others, it was the child's mother who took the initiative by demanding that the offender leave the household.

In those cases where either the child was removed from the home or a parent had left, the sexual activity was generally more serious; the child was more likely to have been injured; the abuse to have gone on for a longer time and to have been more frequent. Data on the types of sexual abuse the child experienced indicate that changes in family constellation (i.e., either a parent leaving

Table 4.9. Involvement of Protective Services and Characteristics of the Sexual Abuse

Relationship with with Offender	N	% involved with protective services before referral to the FCP
Natural parent	30	87%
Parent-figure	32	81%
Other relative	35	54%
Nonfamily	51	45%

Table 4.10. Changes in the Child's Family Constellation as a Consequence of the Sexual Abuse

	N	%
No change in parent figures	85	54%
Child removed	34	22%
Parent left home	37	24%
Totals	156	100%

or the child being removed) were most likely (64%) when the child had been victimized by sexual intercourse (see Table 4.11).

Another important approach to dealing with child sexual abuse involves resorting to police action to apprehend and later prosecute the offender. Sexual contact with children constitutes a clear violation of criminal law. However, not all sexual abuse is reported to the police. In this sample, 33% of the cases included some involvement with the police before coming to the FCP. The decision to involve the criminal justice system in sex abuse cases is complex. A family may seek assistance from the police if they feel that the offender presents a continuing danger to them or if they feel that he should be punished. Theoretically, protective service workers should call upon the criminal justice system because sexual abuse involves a violation of criminal law. It is noteworthy, however, that 69% of the cases that were seen by protective services were not seen by the police. While this study was underway, the Massachusetts legislature mandated that all serious cases of child abuse

Table 4.11. Relationship Between Type of Sexual Act and Changes in the
Child's Family Constellation

		% of cases in which:		
Sex Act	N	No Changes (N = 85)	Child Removed (N = 34)	Parent Left (N = 37)
Intercourse	43	36%	21%	43%
Other penetration	59	56%	27%	17%
Fondling	36	64%	14%	22%
Attempts, nontouching	10	56%	33%	11%

be reported to the appropriate district attorney. Such collaborations
apparently were not occurring during the study period. Indeed,
the police were most often involved at the request of families of
the victims. There was a slight tendency to find greater police
involvement (48% of the cases) when the offender was not a family
member. Further, police were called in more often when the child
came from a white or a two-parent family. Perhaps these families
were more likely to view the police as a source of help than those
headed by a single or a nonwhite parent.

CONCLUSIONS

A description of the sexual abuse experienced by children in
the FCP includes a broad range of experiences, encompassing a
single encounter with an exhibitionist to years of repeated
intercourse with a parent. The distribution of abuse in this sample
suggests that not all sexual activity is equally likely to lead to clinical
intervention. Despite indications that encounters with exhibitionists
are relatively frequent in the general population (Finkelhor, 1979),
few families sought treatment for children who encountered this
experience. One might expect that decisions about seeking or
providing clinical services are closely linked with both parents' and
professionals' assumptions about what constitutes a serious sexual
assault. Thus, it is not surprising that the frequency of types of

sexual abuse treated in the FCP corresponded reasonably close with staff rankings of the seriousness of each type of abuse. The FCP was likely to see more children who had serious sexual experiences than those who had experienced less serious assaults.

In many respects, the types of sexual abuse that occurred most often in this sample reinforce current clinical knowledge about sexual abuse. Old stereotypes that child sexual abuse is committed by "dirty old men" who prey on unfamiliar children in school yards were not confirmed by the data (Groth, Burgess, Birnbaum, & Gary, 1978). The majority of offenders were young adults or adolescents. Most children in this study were victimized by someone they knew quite well, with the majority of children subjected to repeated sexual assaults.

These findings raise questions about conceptions of sexual abuse that have prevailed at one time or another. For example, there had been some tendency in the past to believe that children are often seduced into sexual activity, that they allegedly passively comply with an adult's overtures because of their own needs for attention or affection (DeFrancis, 1969). The present findings suggest that more sexual assaults on children may be overtly aggressive. In almost 55% of the cases, the offender used some form of threat or aggression to gain the child's compliance. Thus, the notion that child sexual abuse typically involves gentle seduction is seriously challenged. Children most often comply with sexual offenders because they are afraid to refuse. What they fear may range from loss of the offender's affection to physical violence. However, it would be unreasonable to suggest that a child is willingly complying with sexual activity if she believes that her father or uncle will not love her any more if she does not do what he says. Perhaps the most striking finding on the role of aggression in child sexual abuse is that family members are just as likely to resort to violence as offenders who are not related to the child.

The findings also provide insight into the issues of keeping the abuse secret. Previous investigators have suggested that few children tell anyone that they have been sexually abused (Finkelhor, 1979). In this study, the most common reason that the sexual abuse was discovered was that a child told about it. These findings suggest that unless a child tells about the abuse the likelihood that it will be discovered by some other means is not especially high.

Thus, it is particularly important to understand the circumstances that enable children to tell others that they have been sexually assaulted. The data suggest that a number of factors may be involved. Children may be more likely to reveal their experiences if they feel less loyalty to the offender. They may have an intuitive understanding about whether they are likely to be believed and whether telling will halt the abuse. It is noteworthy that children usually select parents or relatives as confidants. They are not likely to reveal their experience to outsiders, such as teachers, police, or social workers. Perhaps, children feel that people outside the family could not effectively intercede.

Information on the ways in which sexual abuse is revealed has important implications for developing strategies to increase the disclosure of abuse. Educational programs for children should be designed to assure children that they are permitted to talk about their experiences to responsible adults. This is especially important for victims of incest, who sometimes may perceive correctly that revealing the abuse to a parent may not bring help. Parents should be trained to respond appropriately when a child does raise the topic of sexual assault. As will be noted in the following chapters, not all mothers of victimized children are prepared immediately to offer comfort and protection when they initially discover their children have been abused, and this has important implications for understanding the impact of the abuse on the victim.

NOTE

1. The data forms allowed detailed data for up to three offenders. Although only eight cases were found in which there were three offenders, it is possible that some of these children had been victimized by more than three offenders.

The Effects of Child Sexual Abuse

Coauthored with
MARIA SAUZIER,
PATRICIA SALT,
and ROBERTA CALHOUN

This chapter focuses on the effects of sexual abuse and its disclosure at the time the child entered the Family Crisis Program. Because eligibility criteria required that the abuse or its disclosure have taken place no more than six months prior to treatment, the data presented in this chapter deal with the initial effects of child sexual abuse. Whether the long-term effects would differ from these results is difficult to determine. Longitudinal studies of the impact of child sexual abuse are unavailable. In Chapter 7, follow-up data on the effects of the abuse 18 months after treatment at FCP will be presented, but even these results cannot predict what might happen over the long run as the children reach adulthood and are exposed to new challenges and tragedies. Presentation of the FCP results is preceded by an overview of earlier studies on the effects of sexual abuse.

Sexual Abuse and Emotional
Distress: An Overview

Whether children who have been sexually abused suffer from long-or short-term emotional damage is a topic of considerable debate (Bagley & Ramsey, 1986; Briere, 1987; Browne & Finkelhor, 1986; Conte & Berliner, 1987; Friedrich, 1986; Gomes-Schwartz, Horowitz, & Sauzier, 1985; Sirles, Smith, & Kusama, 1989). This controversy may, to some extent, reflect differences in the populations studied or the methods used to evaluate emotional stress. Two early studies, which drew upon a large sample of adults from the general population, indicated that less than 5% of those who had been sexually abused as children believed the incident had a serious, negative impact on their lives (Gagnon, 1965; Landis, 1956). In a similar sample of adult women, however, 66% suggested that at the time the abuse occurred, the experience had been severely emotionally distressing (Finkelhor, 1979). These surveys are somewhat limited in that they selected for *normal* adults, individuals who were functioning well in their communities; most were attending or had graduated from college. Thus, those victims of sexual abuse who may have suffered the greatest psychological harm—those who were subsequently hospitalized, jailed, or went on to maintain marginal life styles as prostitutes or drug addicts— would have been excluded.

An alternative approach relies upon the examination of individuals who seek clinical services later in life. Such studies suggest a greater incidence of serious emotional harm among those who were sexually victimized as children (Bagley & Ramsey, 1986; Briere & Runtz, 1987; Finkelhor, 1984; Murphy et al., 1988; Russell, 1986). Numerous investigators have described antisocial behavior, including prostitution and drug and alcohol abuse, in adults who have been sexually victimized as children (Benward & Densen-Gerber, 1973; Conte & Schuerman, 1987; Fields, 1981; Giarreto, 1976; James & Meyerding, 1977; Lukianowicz, 1972; Silbert & Pines, 1981). Symptoms of emotional distress such as depression, poor self-esteem, and sexual dysfunction have also been commonly observed (Bagley & Ramsey, 1986; Boekelheide, 1978; Herman, 1981; Meiselman, 1978; Summit & Kryso, 1978; Tsai & Wagner, 1978).

The extent to which sexual abuse in childhood contributed to the psychopathology observed in the adults of these retrospective surveys is difficult to determine. Symptoms of sexual dysfunction are reported so consistently that there is good reason to believe that this problem may have its genesis in the sexual abuse. Contrasts of the rates of sexual abuse in *pathological* versus *normal* populations, as described in James and Meyerding's 1977 study of prostitutes, and the rates of symptoms in incest victims versus psychiatric patients (Meiselman, 1978), also suggest some link between sexual abuse in childhood and emotional disturbances as an adult.

Just as surveys of normal populations select out the most seriously disturbed victims, clinical studies of adults exclude those individuals who do not experience sufficient emotional distress to seek psychiatric care. A third approach to studying the effects of childhood sexual abuse involves examining children as soon as they have been identified as victims or shortly after they have been evaluated (Conte & Schuerman, 1987; Cupoli & Sewell, 1988; McLeer et al., 1988; Mian, Wehrspann, Klajner-Diamond, LeBaron, & Winder, 1986). This research strategy is likely to yield somewhat broader samples of victims than studies of adults who seek treatment voluntarily. Sexually abused children reach medical, psychiatric, or social services because they manifest overt behavioral problems or because someone else, usually a parent or institutional authority figure, believes that the incident necessitates some form of professional intervention.

Clinical reports describing sexually abused children of various ages have highlighted a broad spectrum of symptoms related to emotional distress. Table 5.1 lists some of the most commonly cited symptoms and the studies in which they appeared. These symptoms can be grouped into four broad categories: (1) manifestly inappropriate behaviors that identify the child as both disturbed and disturbing to others (e.g., sexual promiscuity, delinquent activity); (2) somatic expressions of psychological conflict; (3) internalized emotional distress, which may not necessarily be expressed through overt behavioral problems (e.g., feelings of guilt or responsibility for the sexual activity); and (4) diminished self-esteem.

Some clinicians working with children have argued that nearly all sexually abused children exhibit symptoms of emotional distress that are at least as severe as those of other children receiving psychiatric treatment (Adams-Tucker, 1982; Friedrich, Beilke, & Urquiza, 1987; Nakashima & Zakus, 1979). Others have contended that symptoms either subside relatively quickly (Yorukoglu & Kemph, 1969) or are attributable to more long-standing psychiatric problems (Bender & Grugett, 1952). Most investigators agree, however, that the degree to which a child is emotionally harmed and the way in which the child is most likely to express emotional distress are influenced by the child's prior history and current developmental level, as well as the nature of the sexual abuse (Finkelhor, 1987; Lewis & Sarrel, 1969; MacVicar, 1979).

Clinicians and researchers have examined the effects of certain aspects of the sexual activity (e.g., type of sex act, frequency, duration, and relationship with offender), the circumstances surrounding the abuse (e.g., age of the child when sexual contact first occurred, method of gaining compliance), and the factors relating to the revelation of the abuse (e.g., whether the child told about the abuse, how family and institutions responded). Several of these aspects have been implicated repeatedly as predictors of the degree of stress children experience.

The importance of the child's age at initial traumatization as a predictor of psychopathology has generated considerable clinical debate (Lewis & Sarrel, 1969; MacFarlane, 1978; Summit & Kryso, 1978). The question considered in these reports is whether a child is more severely affected when the initial abuse occurs at a very young age or when the child is older (Bagley & Ramsey, 1986; Meiselman, 1978; Russell, 1986). There is some agreement that very young children are less able to comprehend the sexual nature of the experience and hence may show less enduring emotional trauma (Brant & Herzog, 1979; Funk, 1980). Some investigators suggest that the older the child, the greater the probability for emotional damage (Adams-Tucker, 1982; Murphy et al., 1988). One reason for this is that an older child has a greater capacity to

Table 5.1. Symptoms Expressed by Sexually Abused Children
of Different Ages

Pre-School	School-Aged	Adolescent
Anxiety (1,3,5,6)	Anxiety (1,4,5,6)	Anxiety (3)
Withdrawal (5,6)	Withdrawal (1,5,6)	Withdrawal (1)
Guilt (3)	Guilt (4)	Guilt (2)
Somatic complaints/ appetite disturbance (3,5,6)	Somatic complaints/ appetite disturbance (3,5,6)	Somatic complaints (3,4)
Sleep problems/ nightmares (3,5,6)	Sleep problems/ nightmares (3,4)	Sleep problems/ nightmares (4)
Conversion hysteria (3)	Conversion hysteria (5)	
Sexualized behaviors (3,5)	Sexualized behaviors (4,5)	Sexualized behaviors (4)
Regression (3,5)		
Hyperactivity (5)		
Impaired trust (3)		
Lying (3)		
Difficulty separating (7)		
	Depression (1,5)	Depression (1,3,4)
Phobias (6)	Phobias (3,4,5)	Phobias (4)
	School problems (3,4,5)	School problems (4,6)
	Running away (5)	Running away (6)
	Drug abuse (5)	Drug abuse (4,6)
	Suicide attempts (5)	Suicide attempts (4)
	Tics (5)	Tics (7)
	Borderline states (3)	Borderline states (4)
	Aggression (4)	Aggression (1)
	Delinquency/acting-out behavior disorders (1,3,4,5)	Delinquency/acting-out behavior disorders (3,4)
	Obsessions (3,5)	
	Psychosis (6)	
		Lowered self-esteem (3)
		Homosexuality (3,4)
		Hostility (4)
		Disrupted peer relations (6)

(1) Adams-Tucker, 1982; (2) Finkelhor, 1979; (3) Lewis and Sarrel, 1969; (4) MacVicar, 1979; (5) Pascoe and Duterte, 1981; (6) Peters, 1976; (7) Rosenfeld, Nadelson and Krieger, 1979.

understand societal taboos about sexuality and hence to feel more
violated by the assault or more responsible for its occurrence

(Finkelhor, 1979; Nakashima & Zakus, 1977; Summit & Kryso, 1978). Further, the period of adolescence is one in which the sense of autonomy and independence, as well as sexual drives, is developing. Thus adolescents, who may be more likely to question whether they have implicitly complied with the abuse, are particularly prone to suffering guilt and self-recrimination. In contrast, MacVicar (1979) has suggested that adolescents may have a greater capacity than school-aged children to master their trauma.

Some findings have been inconsistent, but suggest that the impact of age at abuse may be influenced by several variables. Adams-Tucker (1982) indicated that age at first molestation did not show a straightforward relationship with severity of pathology. She found that the impact of the abuse was greatest both (1) in children who had initially been abused at an early age and in whom the abuse had continued for a long time, and (2) in those victims who were first abused in adolescence, regardless of the duration. Others (Benward & Densen-Gerber, 1973; Finkelhor, 1979) found the age discrepancy between victim and offender to be more predictive than the age at first victimization (i.e., the greater the age discrepancy, the greater the harm). Tsai, Feldman-Summers, and Edgar (1979) reported that the age of the child when the abuse ended was a better discriminator of adult dysfunction than the age at which the abuse commenced.

A further issue that has generated debate is the significance of the relationship between the child and the offender in influencing distress (e.g., Groth, 1978). The suggestion that father-child incest carries more impact than other types of molestation has been supported by findings in several studies (Adams-Tucker, 1982; Finkelhor, 1979; Lukianowicz, 1972; McLeer et al., 1988; Russell, 1986), but no straightforward connection between the closeness of the relationship (i.e., nuclear family versus relative versus friend versus strangers) and its effect on the child has been established (Finkelhor, 1979).

Some researchers suggest that the duration of the abuse influences stress. The suggestion by Groth (1978) that the longer the experience goes on, the greater the harm to the child, has been supported in studies of adults who were molested during childhood (Brunold, 1964; Gagnon, 1965; Tsai et al., 1979). Other data based on adult recollections of childhood abuse (Finkelhor, 1979) or on evaluations of children (Adams-Tucker, 1982) lend no support to this theory.

Data on the relationship between the type of sexual act (e.g., intercourse, fondling, exhibitionism) and the impact on the child do suggest some hierarchy of seriousness. Tsai et al. (1979) indicated that the presence or absence of intercourse was the crucial distinction, while Adams-Tucker (1982) suggested that children who experienced any genital molestation fared worse. Other investigators have suggested that the degree of violence associated with the abuse is far more important than the sexual act itself (Bagley & Ramsey, 1986; Finkelhor, 1979; Gagnon, 1965; MacVicar, 1979; Peters, 1976; Russell, 1986).

The reactions of others when sexual abuse is first disclosed may also have an important impact upon the child. While some authors suggest it is the pressure to keep the abuse secret that creates the greatest stress for the child (Burgess & Holmstrom, 1975; MacFarlane, 1978), others indicate that telling about sexual abuse, which often evokes strong negative reactions from parents and social agencies, is a source of great stress (Brunold, 1964; Goldstein et al., 1979; Summit & Kryso, 1978). Several investigators note that victims who do not have parental support are more likely to evidence emotional distress (Giaretto, 1981; Lewis & Sarrel, 1969; Peters, 1976; Tsai et al., 1979), while Goldstein et al. (1979) suggest that the attempts of social agencies to protect victimized children by removing them from the home may be even more harmful than leaving a child in an inadequate home environment.

The controversy surrounding these issues may, in part, be attributable to the subjective quality that characterized the evaluation of cases. When clinical cases are categorized by subjective, highly inferential criteria, differences between one therapist's observations and those of another may arise from a variety of factors unrelated to the child's overt behaviors. For example, differences in the clinician's theoretical framework will influence the types of signs, symptoms, or behaviors that are the primary focus of the therapy. Moreover, different labels are often used to describe same or similar behaviors. Actions that one therapist would judge indicative of severe anxiety might be viewed less seriously by another, while a third observer may attribute the same behavior to influences other than sexual abuse (see Wyatt & Peters, 1986). The goal of the present study was to systematically evaluate signs of emotional distress and factors in the child's experience that are associated with levels of distress. This was accomplished by establishing a broad sample of sexually abused children and assessing their psychological functioning with standardized measures of childhood health and psychopathology. The measures selected for this purpose had already been validated with large samples of children in assessing psychological functioning within the four broad categories addressed in previous studies: (1) overt behavior; (2) somaticized reactions; (3) internalized emotional states; and (4) self-esteem.

CRITERIA FOR MEASURING EMOTIONAL DISTRESS

One important aspect of assessing the extent to which children are harmed by sexual abuse is to determine whether the victimized children demonstrate significantly more or different signs of emotional distress than observed in children from the general population or in those receiving treatment for a broad spectrum of psychiatric problems. Because the design of this study did not permit the selection of a demographically matched control group, FCP relied upon data from normative samples, evaluated during the construction and validation of standardized tests. The use of normative data as a basis for comparing the present sample of sexually abused children with other children in the general population or in psychiatric treatment is far from ideal. Even when a standardized test has been carefully constructed with data from very large samples, it is likely that the subjects in the standardization samples do not exactly approximate the characteristics of the broader population to which the testers wish to generalize. Systematic biases in the standardization data are even more of an issue if the standardization sample is small or if data has been collected from "convenient" samples, such as all the children treated in one particular clinic. Nonetheless, comparison of the group of sexually abused children treated by FCP with population norms provides a rough approximation of their relative degree of psychopathology.

Normative data were available for the Louisville Behavior Checklist, the Piers-Harris Self-Concept Scale, the Purdue Self-Concept Scale, and the Gottschalk-Gleser Content Analysis Scales. Relevant characteristics of these scales are summarized here briefly. The Louisville Behavior Checklist is a true-false questionnaire completed by the parents, which addresses childhood behavioral problems. The measure includes three versions: E-1 for 4- to 6-year-olds; E-2 for 7- to 13-year-olds; and E-3 for 14- to 18-year-olds. The E-1 and E-2 versions have norms based upon both a general population and a clinical population drawn from the rolls of child psychiatric clinics. Both versions of the instrument have an overall measure of severity of pathology (Severity Level), and 18 comparable scales (including a measure of somatic problems) are derived from factor analyses of the normative data for each group. The E-3 version is normed only against a clinical population. Although the overall measure of Severity Level in the E-3 version is comparable to that of E-1 and E-2, the 12-factor scales are conceptually different from those derived from the younger age groups. Thus, severity level based on clinical norms was the only measure available for the entire age range.

Positive self-esteem was measured by the Piers-Harris Children's Self-Concept Scale (ages 7-18) or the Purdue Self-Concept for Preschool Children (ages 3-6). Each of these measures have been normed against samples from the general population. Standardized scores from the two measures were combined to obtain an index of self-concept applicable to the entire age range. The children's affective states were assessed with the Gottschalk-Gleser Content Analysis Scales that tap anxiety and hostility. These measures were derived from five-minute speech samples, elicited from the child by the standard open-ended request "tell me a story about yourself." Norms have been obtained for both black and white children, from kindergarten through high school (Gottschalk, Uliana, & Holgard, 1979). The level of anxiety and hostility expressed by the child was assessed through five scales: (1) Total Anxiety; (2) Hostility Directed Outward (i.e., direct expression of hostile wishes or acts toward others); (3) Hostility Directed Inward (i.e., self-blame, despair, and suicidal ideation); (4) Ambivalent Hostility, (i.e., a sum of the three dimensions of hostility); and (5) Total Hostility (i.e., thoughts or focus of others harming the self). Each measure was collected on children 4 years of age and older immediately upon entering the treatment program. As mentioned previously, data could not be obtained for all subjects. Those who were assessed, however, appeared to be representative of the entire sample. They did not differ from the children who were not tested with regard to any aspect of the sexual abuse or important demographic characteristics described in Chapter 3.

The degree of emotional distress manifested through these measures cannot be attributed solely to sexual abuse. Many other factors in the child's history may predispose him or her to exhibit behavioral problems or to experience emotionally painful feelings. The following pages address the issues of: (1) whether sexually abused children exhibit more emotional problems than normal children, and what proportion of children would have been identified as needing clinical services, even if the occurrence of sexual abuse had not been known, and (2) what factors in the child's sexual abuse experience appear to be associated with greater psychopathology.

Because versions of Louisville Behavior Checklist require dividing the sample into three age groups, preschool, school age and adolescents, the issue of the relationship between the child's age and level of distress is presented first. Subsequent analyses examine the impact of factors in the sex abuse situation after the age of the victim was taken into account.

Distress in Preschool Children

Comparison of the FCP sample of 30 children aged 4-6 with similar aged children in the general population indicated that the sexually abused group exhibited significantly more overall behavioral disturbances (see Table 5.2). Although differences were not evident for all aspects of psychopathology, the sexually abused group scored higher on a majority of the dimensions (11 of 18) measured by the Louisville Behavior Checklist. On the other hand, comparison of the sexually abused children with a standard group receiving child psychiatric services indicated that the sexually abused group exhibited less overall pathology and fewer specific difficulties on 15 of 18 scales. On only one dimension, inappropriate sexual behavior, did the sexually victimized group display more difficulties. These results suggest that, as a group, sexually abused preschool children may manifest more problems than their *normal* peers. However, not all of these children displayed behavior sufficiently deviant to suggest to parents or other adults that they were in need of psychiatric intervention.

Miller (1981), who developed the Louisville Behavior Checklist, has suggested that children who score higher than would be expected from 93% of the normal population are very likely to be judged as seriously disturbed. As illustrated in Table 5.2, the proportion of sexually abused preschool children who score in the seriously disturbed range is relatively low. Overall, only 17% of the youngsters meet the criteria for clinically significant psychopathology. In some specific areas, however, greater numbers of sexually abused children demonstrated problems. One-third of the group manifested high levels of behaviors that rarely occur in normal youngsters, such as cruelty to animals, fear of toilets, or fecal smearing (Rare Deviance). As this scale also includes an item signifying that the child has had inappropriate sexual relations, however, one might assume that being sexually abused accounts for many of the elevated scores. Similarly, 27% of the sexually abused children showed high levels of Sexual Behavior, which included both having sexual relations and displaying inappropriate sexual behavior such as open masturbation, excessive sexual curiosity, and/or frequent exposure of the genitals. It is not easy to dismiss this finding as an artifact of the scale composition, because the level of severity on the scale was so high. Also, a second measure of the child's sexual preoccupation from the Child Behavior

Table 5.2. Louisville Behavior Checklist
E-1 (4- to 6-year-olds)

Louisville Scales (N = 30)	Mean	(SD)	Sample significantly differs from general population	Sample significantly differs from clinical population	Percent of sample with clinically significant pathology[3]
Infantile Aggression	54.90	(10.60)	+[1]	−[2]	13%
Hyperactivity	52.43	(9.44)		−	13%
Antisocial Behavior	53.70	(11.29)		−	13%
Aggression	56.03	(13.81)	+	−	17%
Social Withdrawal	51.10	(9.10)		−	10%
Sensitivity	55.17	(8.05)	+	−	7%
Fear	55.50	(9.87)	+	−	13%
Inhibition	54.77	(8.05)	+	−	10%
Intellectual Deficit	52.27	(12.04)		−	17%
Immaturity	56.80	(10.61)	+	−	23%
Cognitive Disability	55.10	(11.23)	+	−	20%
Normal Irritability	52.40	(6.77)		−	3%
Prosocial Deficit	54.40	(10.33)	+	−	20%
Rare Deviance	64.53	(16.62)	+		33%
Neurotic Behavior	56.53	(11.69)	+	−	20%
Psychotic Behavior	52.73	(8.99)			10%
Somatic Behavior	53.17	(10.44)		−	13%
Sexual Behavior	63.70	(15.71)	+	+	27%
Severity Level	55.40	(9.53)	+	−	17%

1. + indicates that sample mean is significantly greater ($p < .05$) than normative mean using t-test for a single sample.
2. − indicates that sample mean is significantly less ($p < .05$) than normative mean using t-test for a single sample.
3. Clinically significant = 1.5 SD greater than the mean for the general population.

Checklist developed at Children's Hospital (Washington, D.C.) suggests that serious age inappropriate sexual activity is one of the more common symptoms seen in our preschool sexual abuse victims.

The observation that inappropriate sexual behavior is one of the most common symptoms in preschool youngsters may offer some insight into the ways in which a cognitively immature child attempts to process an incomprehensible experience. Repeated imitations with peers of sexual behaviors initiated by adults, sometimes represent attempts by youngsters to gain mastery over the confusing feelings that were aroused by the sexual stimulation. In other instances, a child's repetition of sexual acts may represent an identification with the aggressor. In some cases, where the offender neither frightened nor physically harmed the child, the child may not express any conscious awareness that the sexual activity was wrong. Indeed, some children may repeat the activities because the stimulation prematurely awakened sexual drives and was found to be pleasurable. However, other very young children seem to be acutely aware that the offender's behavior was inappropriate. For example, upon hearing that a regular babysitter would not be staying with her, one 4-year-old girl expressed relief that she would not have to "play those dirty games anymore."

Other scales on which considerable portions of children obtained elevated scores indicated both deficits in development and reactions to stress. A total of 22% of the youngsters showed serious deficits in intellectual, physical, and social development (Cognitive Disability). A comparable number lacked the social skills that are usually ingrained during early development, such as a sense of right and wrong (Prosocial Deficit). Symptoms of immaturity, which were marked in 23% of the group, could either reflect failure to attain age appropriate motor and social skills, or regression to more childish behaviors because of stress. The severe anxieties, fears, or depression (Neurotic Behavior) displayed by 20% of the children are more clearly symptoms that reflect responses to emotionally traumatic experiences.

The relatively high incidence of behavior indicative of developmental delay in sexually abused preschoolers raises interesting questions about handicaps or disabilities that may increase one's vulnerability to sexual abuse. It is unlikely that the immaturity or lack of awareness of social norms observed in some of the youngest victims was purely a reaction to the sexual experience. It is more probable that many of these youngsters had longstanding developmental difficulties that made them easier prey for sexual offenders. Because of intellectual handicaps or difficulties in developing relationships with people, some children may have less capacity to recognize deviations from socially acceptable behavior.

Thus, they are less capable of defending themselves against sexual advances and may be less likely to report the incident immediately.

The extent to which these sexually abused children were experiencing stressful affects at the time they entered the clinic was determined by comparing Gottschalk scores with norms for the general population and determining the proportion of cases that exhibited affect scores in the top 7% of a normal population (see Table 5.3).

Hostility levels were substantially elevated in 20% to 25% of the sample. The group, as a whole, did not differ from children in the general population. Only 5% of the sexually abused preschool children exhibited high levels of anxiety in conversation. Indeed, average manifest anxiety was lower than that of *normal* children. Similarly unexpected findings were obtained on the Purdue Self-Concept Scale; the sexually abused children exhibited a more positive self-concept than the normative population.

Effects on School-Age Children

Comparison of the 58 sexually abused 7- to 13-year-olds with the same age group in the general population indicated that the victims of sexual abuse exhibited significantly more psychopathology in every area except bodily complaints (Somatic Behavior) and lack of socially valued interpersonal skills (Prosocial Deficit). When the sexually abused sample was contrasted with a population of school-age children undergoing psychiatric care, the results were similar to those obtained with preschool youngsters. The sexual abuse victims were less disturbed than other children in treatment on a majority of dimensions (13 of 18). Only in the area of inappropriate Sexual Behavior did they exhibit higher degrees of disturbance (see Table 5.4).

As noted previously, not all of the youngsters who were sexually abused manifested extreme or obvious emotional disturbances. The FCP accepted Miller's (1981) criterion, that a child who scores higher than 93% of normal children is very likely to be perceived by others as being seriously disturbed, and calculated the proportion of

Table 5.3. Self-Concept and Affective States in 4- to 6-Year-Olds

Scale	Mean	(SD)	Sample significantly differs from normal population	Percent of sample with clinically significant[4] deviation from normal
Gottschalk (N = 20)				
Anxiety	44.61	(9.00)	–[2]	5%
Hostility Directed Outward	54.77	(17.20)		25%
Hostility Directed Inward	52.57	(18.06)		20%
Ambivalent Hostility	53.19	(22.64)		20%
Total Hostility	53.51	(12.98)		25%
Purdue Self-Concept[1] (N = 31)	54.38	(9.36)	+[3]	3%

1. Higher scores indicate better self-concept.
2. – indicates that sample mean is significantly less ($p < .05$) than normative mean using t-test for a single sample.
3. + indicates that sample mean is significantly greater ($p < .05$) than normative mean using t-test for a single sample.
4. Clinically significant = 1.5 SD greater than the mean for the general population (Gottschalk scores) or 1.5 SD less than the mean (Self-Concept scores).

children who demonstrated elevated scores on each scale. Overall, 40% of the school-aged youngsters were seriously disturbed. The types of symptoms that occurred most frequently (i.e., in 45% or more of the group) were somewhat different from those that had been observed in preschool children. As with preschool children, unusual deviant behaviors were quite common (Rare Deviance, 76%); however, this finding can also be explained by inclusion in the scale of items that assess whether the child had had sexual contact. Other common symptom patterns seemed to reflect angry, destructive behavior or more internalized anxieties. Close to half of the youngsters showed serious difficulties on each of three scales measuring aspects of aggression, including impulsivity (Aggression, 45%), belligerent self-centered behavior (Infantile Aggression, 50%), and illegal, destructive behavior (Antisocial Behavior, 45%). In all, 45% also showed severe fears in response to a broad range of situations (Fear). In addition to those problems, substantial portions

Table 5.4. Louisville Behavior Checklist
E-2 (7- to 13-year-olds)

Louisville Scale (N = 58)	Mean	(SD)	Sample significantly differs from general population	Sample significantly differs from clinical population	Percent sample with clinically significant pathology[3]
Infantile Aggression	65.59	(19.76)	+[1]	–[2]	50%
Hyperactivity	58.62	(14.16)	+	–	28%
Antisocial Behavior	67.57	(25.58)	+	–	45%
Aggression	64.45	(18.75)	+	–	45%
Social Withdrawal	56.31	(12.73)	+	–	18%
Sensitivity	60.26	(14.71)	+	–	38%
Fear	64.26	(17.01)	+		45%
Inhibition	61.09	(15.13)	+	–	36%
Academic Disability	58.10	(11.98)	+		31%
Immaturity	64.05	(19.27)	+	–	40%
Learning Disability	61.11	(13.95)	+		29%
Normal Irritability	52.88	(9.86)	+	–	12%
Prosocial Deficit	40.91	(15.87)	–	–	12%
Rare Deviance	88.79	(30.13)	+	–	76%
Neurotic Behavior	62.60	(21.19)	+	–	38%
Psychotic Behavior	54.12	(14.55)	+	–	19%
Somatic Behavior	51.69	(15.35)		–	16%
Sexual Behavior	61.72	(25.33)	+	+	36%
Severity Level	64.63	(19.85)	+	–	40%

1. – indicates that sample mean is significantly less ($p < .05$) than normative mean using t-test for a single sample.
2. + indicates that sample mean is significantly greater ($p < .05$) than normative mean using t-test for a single sample.
3. Clinically significant = 1.5 SD greater than the mean for the general population.

of school-age children also displayed pathology on some of the scales that had distinguished the younger children: Sexual Behavior (36%), Neurotic Behavior (38%), Immaturity (40%). The failure to acquire socially valued behaviors (Prosocial Deficit), a characteristic of the younger children, was not an issue for many of the school-age youngsters. On the contrary, as a group, they exhibited fewer difficulties in this area than normal children. Another unexpected finding was that relatively few of the school-aged children exhibited serious somatic complaints (16%). This is contrary to a number of clinical observations that sexually abused children often complain of headaches or stomachaches.

Stressful affects present at the time the children entered treatment were variable (Table 5.5). Only 11% exhibited high levels of anxiety and 17% showed substantial self-directed hostility (Hostility Directed Inward). However, 35% expressed high levels of anger toward others (Hostility Directed Outward) and 41% expressed concerns about harm from others (Ambivalent Hostility). On both of these dimensions, as well as Total Hostility, the sexually abused children demonstrated higher scores than normative populations. With respect to Self-Concept this sample did not differ from children in the general population (Table 5.5).

Effects on Adolescents

Because the Louisville version (E-3) for 14- to 18-year-olds was normed only against a clinical population, it was impossible to contrast the 25 sexually abused youths with normal adolescents. Comparisons of the sample with adolescents in psychiatric treatment yielded data consistent with those from the younger subjects. On 10 of 13 scales, sexually abused adolescents were less pathological compared with other adolescents in treatment (Table 5.6).

Assessing whether a particular youth is seriously disturbed is more complex when the only comparison group includes other disturbed youths. Miller (1981) suggests a rather strict criterion for judging serious disturbance under these circumstances; namely, the individual must score higher than 69% of the population in treatment. Given this criterion, relatively small portions of the sexually abused adolescents exhibited severe pathology on most scales. However, 24% displayed significant Neuroticism, a measure of anxiety, depression, and obsessive concerns; and 21% displayed Dependent-Inhibited behavior, including lack of self-confidence.

As illustrated in Table 5.7, the most prevalent stressful feelings among the adolescents involved fears of being harmed (Ambivalent Hostility, 36% elevated) and overt anger (Hostility Directed

Table 5.5. Self-Concept and Affective States in 7- to 13-Year-Olds

Scale	Mean	(SD)	Sample significantly differs from population	Percent of sample with clinically significant deviation from normal[3]
Gottschalk (N = 46)				
Anxiety	48.10	(12.77)		11%
Hostility Directed Outward	58.60	(18.35)	+[2]	35%
Hostility Directed Inward	52.65	(13.03)		17%
Ambivalent Hostility	57.56	(22.16)	+	41%
Total Hostility	56.26	(13.92)	+	28%
Piers-Harris Self-Concept (N = 65)[1]	51.91	(9.48)		3%

1. Higher scores indicate better self-concept.
2. + indicates that sample mean is significantly greater ($p < .05$) than normative mean using t-test for a single sample.
3. Clinically significant = 1.5 SD greater than the mean for the general population (Gottschalk scores) or 1.5 SD less than the mean (Self-Concept scores).

Outward, 23% elevated). Only on Total Hostility did the adolescents manifest significantly higher scores than the normative population. Results for Self-Concept were comparable to those obtained with younger children; very small proportions (4%) deviated from the norm in a pathological direction.

There are several possible explanations for this finding of low levels of pathology in adolescent victims. As MacVicar (1979) has suggested, perhaps those who are first victimized in adolescence are better able to cognitively process the experience. In fact, several of the adolescent girls identified as victims experienced the sexual contact as consensual. For example, a 13-year-old girl who engaged in intercourse with her 21-year-old uncle perceived him as her boyfriend and could not understand her mother's distress when the sexual activity was disclosed.

Another possibility is that some of the more seriously disturbed victims were not treated at the FCP. As noted previously, adolescent male victims are less likely to seek help than females. In fact, most of the adolescent boys seen at the FCP were referred because they had been sexual aggressors. Although more than half had also

Table 5.6. Louisville Behavior Checklist
E-3 (14- to 18-year-olds)

Louisville Scale (N = 25)	Mean	(SD)	Sample significantly differs from clinical population	Percent sample with clinically significant pathology[2]
Egocentric-Exploitive	43.52	(6.40)	–[1]	4%
Destructive-Assaultive	43.52	(6.40)	–	8%
Social Delinquency	42.52	(6.99)	–	8%
Adolescent Turmoil	43.76	(8.75)	–	4%
Apathetic Isolation	48.08	(7.14)		8%
Neuroticism	44.84	(11.53)	–	24%
Dependent-Inhibited	48.13	(10.39)		21%
Academic Disability	40.72	(8.46)	–	4%
Neurological or Psychotic Abnormality	49.16	(7.83)		16%
General Pathology	38.44	(8.57)	–	12%
Longitudinal	41.21	(9.27)	–	8%
Severity Level	41.76	(8.71)	–	8%
Total Pathology	40.56	(9.35)	–	8%

1. – indicates that sample mean is significantly less ($p < .05$) than normative mean using t-test for a single sample.
2. Clinically significant = 0.5 SD greater than the mean for the clinical population.

been sexually victimized earlier in their lives, they did not meet the criteria for the crisis intervention program and hence could not be included in this sample. Perhaps many other adolescents were not accessible to the type of intervention provided in this study because of the severity of their acting out behavior. Such seriously delinquent adolescents are especially likely to fail to cooperate with noncoercive, outpatient psychiatric treatment.

INFLUENCES ON EMOTIONAL DISTRESS

In addition to the child's age when clinical services are received, a number of other factors have been hypothesized as influencing the degree to which a sexually abused child experiences emotional trauma. The following discusses the degree of emotional distress

Table 5.7 Self-Concept and Affective States in 14- to 18-Year-Olds

Scale	Mean	(SD)	Sample significantly differs from general population	Percent of sample with clinically significant deviation from normal[3]
Gottschalk (N = 22)				
Anxiety	48.72	(9.48)		5%
Hostility Directed Outward	55.74	(12.40)		23%
Hostility Directed Inward	54.73	(14.65)		18%
Ambivalent Hostility	58.00	(22.75)		36%
Total Hostility	56.16	(13.19)	+[2]	23%
Piers-Harris Self-Concept				
(N = 27)[1]	49.75	(9.08)		4%

1. Higher scores indicate better self-concept.
2. + indicates that sample mean is significantly greater ($p < .05$) than normative mean using t-test for a single sample.
3. Clinically significant = 1.5 SD greater than the mean for the general population (Gottschalk scores) or 1.5 SD less than the mean (Self-Concept scores).

exhibited by the child upon entering treatment at FCP and the relationship of the distress to: (1) the use of aggression and the extent of physical injury to the child; (2) the nature of the sexual abuse; (3) the duration of the abuse; (4) the child's relationship to the offender; (5) the disclosure of the abuse; (6) the nature of the response by the child's mother to the abuse; and (7) the separation of the child from the parents.

The extent to which the child manifested emotional distress was measured by the Gottschalk Gleser Content-Analysis Scales, the Purdue and Piers-Harris Self-Concept Scales, and the Louisville Behavior Checklist. Data from the Louisville Behavior Checklist scales were reduced to five summary scores. The overall measure of severity of psychopathology was applicable to children of ages 4 through 18. In addition, scores on the Louisville scales for 4- to 13-year-olds were combined into four broad dimensions: (1) overall aggression and antisocial behavior; (2) signs of emotional distress such as fearfulness, withdrawal from contact with others, and inhibited behavior; (3) symptoms of severe psychiatric illness such as fire-setting, inability to distinguish reality from fantasy, or phobias; and (4) problems with school performance and intellectual ability.

The aim of this analysis was to determine the extent to which each aspect of the sexual abuse could explain some of the variability in the degree of psychological disturbance displayed by each child. As it was already determined that the age when the child first entered treatment was related to the degree of manifest behavioral disturbance, analyses were designed to control for the effects of the child's age when initially evaluated. In essence, FCP posed this question: Given that children in the 7 to 13 age range display more distress than younger children, how much of this distress can be accounted for by factors inherent in the sexual abuse? (Details of statistical analyses and tables of data are reported in Appendix B.)

The Use of Aggression and the Nature of Sexual Abuse

Previous findings have suggested that abuse that continues for long periods of time and involves more intrusive sexual acts and greater overt aggression on the part of the perpetrator evokes more distress in a child. The FCP data support only one of these hypotheses. There was a modest degree of association between the amount of violence associated with the abuse and signs of emotional distress in the victimized children. Children who had suffered physical injuries during the sexual abuse were more likely to exhibit behavioral problems in all of the areas measured by the Louisville scales. Additionally, children who were induced to comply with the offender through overt aggression were more likely to express overall hostility on the Gottschalk scales, as well as more fears of aggressive behavior in others (Ambivalent Hostility), than those who were not aggressively approached.

In contrast, there was little indication that particular sexual acts, in and of themselves, influenced trauma. In the hierarchy of seriousness of sex acts agreed upon by the staff of the FCP, intercourse was considered the most harmful sexual activity. There was no indication, however, that children subjected to intercourse suffered any greater stress than those who experienced other sexual acts. Indeed, the only association between the type of activity involved in the abuse and the child's distress was somewhat anomalous. Children who had experienced only fondling expressed the most anxiety on the Gottschalk scales. This finding is difficult to explain. However, the fact that many children who were fondled reported the abuse soon after it happened may provide a clue. Those children who were fondled and immediately told might still have been experiencing the initial shock of being assaulted when they reached the FCP. In contrast, children who had been abused over a longer period of time may have dealt with their feelings in a different fashion.

The finding that violence was a more important influence on a child's reaction than the type of sexual activities is consistent with the literature on rape. As several investigators have suggested (e.g., Burgess, Groth, & Holmstrom, 1974; Groth, Burgess, & Holmstrom, 1977), sexual assaults are primarily expressions of aggression and violence rather than sexual feelings. Thus, it is not surprising that the aggressive component of a sexual assault upon a child is so important. Threatened or actual bodily harm may transform sexual activities from odd or puzzling experiences to terrifying attacks.

Duration of the Sexual Abuse

FCP data also failed to substantiate the hypothesis that abuse that continues over a longer period or that begins earlier in the child's life is necessarily more harmful. No relationship was found between the length of the abuse or the age of the child at the time the abuse first began and the effects of the experience on the child (Browne & Finkelhor, 1986). Although there had been some indication that older preadolescent children showed more problems with school and aggressive behavior, this finding was better explained by their age when first evaluated than by their age when first abused. The absence of a straightforward relationship in this study between the amount of distress a child expressed and the age at which the child was first abused provides some insight into the seemingly contradictory observations previously reported in literature (Adams-Tucker, 1982; MacVicar, 1979). Adolescent victims may manifest different signs of distress than younger children because both the circumstances of their abuse and their concepts of what the abuse might mean are different. However, placing these differing reactions on a continuum of lesser to greater overall distress may not be justifiable.

There are several potential explanations for why the duration of abuse did not appear to be related to the pathology in this study. One possibility is that the level of emotional distress a child evidences when sexual abuse is first revealed may be influenced more by factors in the immediate situation, such as the furor occasioned by the revelation, than by the history of abuse. This does not necessarily mean that long-term adjustment is not influenced by a history of repeated abuse. The child who has experienced long-standing sexual victimization may not appear manifestly symptomatic at intake. Nevertheless, the experience may have had damaging effects on personality development; effects that will only become evident later in life.

It is also possible that the absence of a significant relationship between duration of abuse and psychopathology results from limitations in the study. Perhaps, as Adams-Tucker (1982) has suggested, the duration of the abuse interacts with other factors in affecting the child's adjustment. The FCP sample of subjects was not large enough to permit statistical analyses of the interactions between factors.[1] In addition, as discussed earlier, some more disturbed adolescent victims may be excluded from samples of voluntary outpatient psychiatric cases. Such exclusions could influence the findings if these patients also tended to have been abused for longer periods of time.

Relationships of Child to the Offender

FCP findings provide some support to the concept that abuse by a parental figure is more traumatic than other types of abuse.

Nevertheless, one important distinction not addressed in previous studies was found. Children abused by parent-figures who were not biologically related to them (e.g., stepfathers, boyfriends of mothers) exhibited the lowest self-esteem and the most severe problems with aggression and school performance (see Russell, 1984). There was no indication that children victimized by natural parents were more disturbed than those who were abused by other relatives or persons outside the family. Thus, the crucial variable does not seem to be whether the offender was a father, but whether he was a substitute father. Why sexual abuse at the hands of a parent-surrogate should be more devastating for a child than incest with a father is not completely clear. FCP data indicated that stepfathers were no more likely to be violent than natural fathers. One significant factor may be that more mothers were conflicted in their allegiance when the abuser was someone other than the child's natural father. (As will be discussed in Chapter 6, mothers were especially likely to be unsupportive of children who had been abused by parent-surrogates.) Therefore, the victimized child suffered the double trauma of being exploited by someone he or she may have come to perceive as a protective parental figure and at the same time being rejected by the mother. An alternative possibility is that children with abusive stepfathers may have a more severe history of disruptions in family life. They may have been prone to emotional difficulties even before the sexual abuse occurred because they were poor and had come from an already unstable home environment.

Disclosure of the Sexual Abuse

Findings on the effects of keeping the abuse secret, as opposed to telling, did not support the idea that children who hide the abuse necessarily suffer greater psychic distress. In fact, it was found that children who had not told about the sexual activity before coming to the FCP expressed the least anxious and hostile feelings on the Gottschalk scales (see Appendix B). Interpretation of this result is complex. Perhaps some of the children who were least distressed by the abuse were also least likely to feel a need to report it. As noted in Chapter 4, many of the children who had only minor sexual contacts failed to reveal the abuse themselves. In addition, some children may not have experienced the abuse as especially upsetting or worthy of reporting because they had a limited cognitive understanding of what was happening. This was especially likely in very young children or those with intellectual deficits. An alternative interpretation is that the act of telling about the sexual abuse itself evokes considerable tension. Children who reveal that important people in their lives have misused them may feel considerable anxiety, either because they fear retribution or because they feel guilty about causing disruption in their families.

The Maternal Response to Sexual Abuse

FCP data indicate that a mother's expression of concern about the child and ability to take action to protect her child did not necessarily shield the child from the harmful psychological consequences of the sexual abuse. Positive responses on the part of the mother were not systematically related to the amount of distress the child experienced. However, when a mother expressed anger toward the victimized child and punished that child for revealing the abuse, the child was likely to manifest greater behavioral disturbance (see Appendix B). Furthermore, an angry reaction on the mother's part was associated with lower self-esteem in the child. It is, of course, possible to argue that some of this anger predated the sexual abuse and thereby reflected a response to a child with a history of behavioral problems.

In Chapter 6, it will be shown that mothers who responded to the sexual abuse with anger also tended to have a generally hostile attitude toward their children. It is conceivable that one of the reasons mothers became upset with the victimized child is that the child may have been exhibiting problem behaviors for some time, and the abuse only added to their level of exasperation. An alternative hypothesis is that punitive reactions by mothers might be related to their own cultural background or inadequacy as a parent. Whatever the reason, it is clear that a child who is blamed or punished for revealing sexual abuse is likely to manifest more severe emotional problems.

Removing the Child from the Home

The question of whether children are harmed rather than helped by institutional intervention has been hotly debated. Findings in this study reinforce the idea that removing a sexually abused child from the home may not protect the child from psychological stress. Children who were removed from their homes following the sexual abuse exhibited more overall behavior problems, particularly aggression, than children who either remained with the parents they had lived with when they were abused or who remained with the rest of the family after the parent-perpetrator had been forced to leave (see Appendix B). However, referring again to Chapter 6, it was found that the decision to remove the child from the home seemed to occur more often with mothers who were angry and punitive toward the child. Thus, the extent to which children may already have been traumatized before they were removed from their homes is not clear. Indeed, the decision to remove the child may have been based on the fact that the child was exhibiting severe distress.

CONCLUSIONS

The findings by FCP support the concept that, as a group, children who have recently been sexually abused manifest more behavioral problems and more stressful emotional reactions than children in the general population. It is equally apparent, however, that not all child-victims of sexual abuse demonstrate the severity of symptoms seen in children undergoing psychiatric treatment for a broad range of problems. Instead, the level of psychological distress observed in these youngsters seems to range from a complete absence of any conventional symptoms of childhood psychopathology to the presence of extreme and pervasive emotional problems. Two cases illustrate the dramatic differences observed in children entering the FCP clinic.

Case 1

Susan was an 8-year-old girl who had been subjected to intercourse and oral-genital contact with her mother's live-in boyfriend. Susan reported having trouble sleeping at night, in addition to having nightmares that focused upon themes of aggression, death, and sexuality. At school she had difficulty concentrating and stole small items from other students. In therapy sessions she was whiny, petulant, and immature. Psychological testing indicated that she was extremely disturbed and possessed few adequate coping skills.

Case 2

In contrast, Jan, a 10-year-old girl who had been shown pornography and forced to undress for her natural father, manifested no overt behavioral problems. She was open and friendly in the interviews and talked easily about her sexual experiences. The clinician described her as being a "child who can speak up for herself." Jan felt she could protect herself from further advances by her father, who no longer lived at home. She was discharged without a referral for further treatment at the conclusion of the crisis intervention.

Several potential explanations can be offered for why some children exhibit serious emotional problems while others do not.

The preceding cases illustrate the considerable diversity in the types of sexual experiences, as well as other life experiences, presented by these children. In this regard, the FCP staff attempted to determine which factors in the victim's experiences were consistently associated with greater levels of emotional distress.

The findings confirm some of the hypotheses suggested in the clinical literature and fail to support others. Consistent with previous reports, the age of the child upon entering treatment was an important factor in influencing the degree and type of emotional disturbance that was observed. Relatively few preschool youngsters demonstrated sufficient behavioral problems to be designated as seriously disturbed. This finding is consistent with suggestions made by other investigators (e.g., Funk, 1980) that very young children are less likely to be harmed by sexually abusive experiences because they have little appreciation either of the societal taboo against sexual activity or the consequences of such actions.

In contrast to the low levels of serious emotional disturbance found in preschool children, severe psychological difficulties appear to be quite frequent in youngsters in the 7- to 13-year-old group. One hypothesis is that the older victims are more cognizant of the meaning of sexual approaches and inappropriate sexual activity. It is noteworthy that the older children were also more likely to express both overt anger and fear of being harmed. Differences between preschool and school-aged youngsters would suggest that adolescents who are at an even higher level of cognitive development and are more likely to have been abused for longer periods of time ought to respond most intensely to sexual abuse. It is somewhat surprising, therefore, that so few of the adolescent victims in this study exhibited severe psychopathology.

The differences in predominant patterns of symptoms distinguishing school-aged from adolescent victims may shed some light on the low levels of disturbance observed in the adolescents who were treated at the FCP. School-aged youngsters seemed to be characterized either by internalized anxieties or externalized rage. That is, they were either inhibited by their fears or inclined to express their fury through impulsive, destructive behavior. In contrast, the adolescents fell predominantly into the anxious, inhibited category. One might speculate that victims who began treatment in adolescence were similar to the anxious, fearful school-aged children when they were initially abused. Perhaps because of their fearful reactions, many kept the abuse secret, so that their victimization was not discovered until they were older. In contrast, some of the youngsters who had responded to sexual abuse during their earlier childhood with aggressive behavior might have been less likely to reach a clinic such as the FCP. Their tendency to act upon their feelings might have led them to run away or to be placed in treatment settings for delinquent children before reaching adolescence. The child who responds to sexual abuse at age 8 or 9 through destructive, acting-out behaviors and receives no clinical intervention at that time may become the teenager who turns to prostitution, becomes a sexual abuser of young children, or becomes a perpetrator of other illegal behavior. If the hypothesis that adolescents who cannot be reached through an outpatient treatment service are likely to be similar to those who exhibit antisocial behavior at earlier ages was to be validated, then it would be particularly important to provide clinical services for younger sexual abuse victims before their distress leads to other more severe problems.

Analyses of the impact of aspects of the sexual abuse and reactions by others to the victimized child also yielded mixed findings. Thus, there was clear evidence that the mother's reaction to the abuse was an important factor in understanding the amount of distress the child was experiencing upon entering treatment. The results also confirmed the importance of violence in inducing stress; children who were physically hurt manifested more problems than those who were sexually exploited in a less aggressive fashion. Indeed, it appears that the specific types of sexual acts were much less salient than the degree of violence that accompanied the sexuality. In addition, children who had been removed from their homes were also especially likely to evidence distress.

The influence of other factors was more complex than previous observations had indicated. For example, incest per se was not a predictor of trauma. Instead, important distinctions between types of incest offenders were found. Similarly, there was no straightforward relationship between keeping the abuse secret and suffering more distress. The findings of lesser anxiety and anger among the children who never told about the abuse suggest that revelation of sexual exploitation may not necessarily provide immediate relief; at times it may even exacerbate stress on the child.

Finally, some hypotheses about the sources of stress were totally unsupported by the data. The failure to find any association between duration of the abuse or age of the child at the outset and the child's psychological state must be interpreted with caution. Rather than suggesting that duration of the abuse is not predictive of emotional trauma, the results may perhaps indicate that the relationships between duration and trauma are too complex to be adequately assessed by current methods.

Similarly, the failure to find evidence that sexually abused children, regardless of age, consistently display low self-esteem raises the question of whether clinical hypotheses are indeed unsupported or whether the result is attributable to limitations in the research approach. It is possible that sexual experiences do not necessarily have as pervasive an impact upon a child's sense of self as one might believe. Although many children may be frightened and distressed when they are sexually assaulted, they may not interpret the assault as evidence that they are less worthy or less capable people. An alternative explanation is that scores on self-report measures, such as the Purdue and Piers-Harris self-concept scales, are quite susceptible to a child's effort to deliberately present himself or herself in a positive light. Children who worry that the clinical evaluation in which they are participating will disrupt their families or who indicate that they are to blame for the sexual abuse may be especially prone to "fake good." This same tendency to present the family in the best possible light may also have reduced scores on some of the Louisville Behavior Checklists that parents completed.

It is important to recognize one other limitation inherent in the data. It is not certain to what degree the behavioral disturbances observed after a child has been sexually abused resulted directly from the abuse, as opposed to some predisposing factor that made the child more vulnerable to being sexually abused. Similarly, the data do not enable us to distinguish longstanding difficulties from more recent responses to emotional trauma. Other experiences in the child's history occurring before the sexual abuse may account for some of the psychopathology observed on initial evaluation. For example, FCP found that the overall severity of symptoms measured by the Louisville Behavior Checklist tended to be higher in children at the poverty level, in children who had suffered the loss of a parent figure(s), and in those who had had previous psychiatric treatment.

Despite the limitations in the data and in the complexity of the analyses that were performed, these results have important implications for treatment of sexually abused children. First of all, both these data and the finding that 44% of the children in the study were not referred for continued psychiatric treatment at the conclusion of brief crisis intervention suggests that not all victims of sexual abuse are so emotionally damaged that they require extensive psychiatric treatment. However, the high levels of painful emotions evidenced by many of the subjects suggest that even the victims who did not manifest overt behavior problems were in need of some services to help them deal with their feelings about the abuse as soon as possible after it had occurred.

Early intervention seems to be especially important for children who respond to their victimization by an angry rejection of social norms. The longer such children go without psychological help, the more difficult it may be to engage them effectively in treatment. However, the passive, inhibited responses of other children should not be overlooked. Because such children are less disturbing to the adults around them, they may go untreated for longer periods of time. Yet, they may develop psychic scars that have a significant impact upon their capacity to enjoy stable, fulfilling lives. Indeed, even the children who exhibit no obvious symptoms shortly after the abuse has been revealed may develop difficulties later in life. For example, several investigators (e.g., Briere & Runtz, 1987; Giaretto, 1981; Meiselman, 1978) have observed difficulties with sexuality in adult women who were sexually victimized during childhood. For many of the subjects treated by FCP, the impact of the sexual abuse on adult sexual adjustment will not be apparent for years.

The degree of manifest distress that a child exhibits also has an impact on the way in which treatment should be conducted. In dealing with a young child who exhibits little or no overt symptoms, the clinician does not need to focus exclusively upon reactions to the sexual abuse. In fact, repetitive probing into the details of the sexual experience should be avoided. Instead, treatment might focus on developing the child's understanding of when an adult's approaches are inappropriate and when protection should be sought from a responsible adult. An important aspect of treatment is helping parents to respond appropriately to the victimized child. Their own anxiety may make it difficult for them to provide the child with the calming reassurance needed in order to master the experience.

Helping parents respond supportively to a victimized child is especially important because of the impact that negative maternal reactions appear to have on the child's level of emotional distress. However, it is first necessary to determine why a particular mother has responded angrily to her victimized child and whether her attitude can be successfully modified. The data cannot provide definitive answers, but there are suggestions that a mother's negative reactions may be influenced by a variety of factors, including cultural background, relationship with the offender, and previously demonstrated capacity to care adequately for the child (see Chapter 6). It is important for the clinician to understand the source of a mother's negative reaction. If a mother's background and upbringing reinforce the belief that a child should be punished for "dirty" or "immoral behavior," that mother may need some form of reeducation that emphasizes the child's powerlessness and need for support. Conversely, a mother who experiences a conflict of allegiance between her child and her partner may require more extensive therapeutic intervention before she can fully protect her child. Finally, some mothers who have a history of abusing or neglecting the child prior to the sexual abuse may never be capable of assuming appropriate care of the abused child.

The high levels of psychopathology found in children who were removed from their homes because of the sexual abuse raise important questions about the decision to sever parental responsibility. As noted, it is not possible to determine from the data whether removing a child heightens the child's distress, or whether the child was removed because of the presence of extreme distress. Thus, the crucial issue for protective service and clinical personnel is to determine which course of action will cause the least disruption in the child's life. A preferable alternative to automatically removing a child from the home would be to assist the family in determining whether the child can be protected from further assaults. In some cases, public knowledge of the abuse may provide sufficient restraint on the offender. A father who feels shame and remorse for his behavior may not necessarily pose a threat to his child once his wife and others have been alerted to the sexual behaviors. When clinicians feel that an offender living in the child's home is likely to reabuse that child, arranging for the offender, rather than the child, to leave may be the least disruptive course of action. Finally, in some instances a child's family may be so unable to provide support or protection that the child can only receive adequate care in another setting. As mentioned previously, a child's decision to tell of sexual abuse may evoke considerable anxiety. If this revelation is met with anger or a flurry of activity resulting in unnecessary family disruption, the belief by the child that he or she is at fault may inadvertently be reinforced.

Knowledge that the degree of violence in a sexual assault may be a potent influence on children's reactions also has implications for intervention. Children who have been physically hurt or who have been threatened with bodily harm have good reason to fear that the sexual offender may still hurt them. Thus, one of the tasks of intervention with these children is to ensure that they are safe. It is unclear just how long children's anxieties continue, once they have been protected from further assault. Clinicians may often ascertain through children's play whether they are still fearful of the offender. There is even greater risk of long-term distress when a child is subjected to continued exposure to the offender in either the home or neighborhood.

The present findings about those factors that are likely to increase a child's risk of suffering severe emotional trauma may also assist the clinician in determining how best to allocate scarce treatment resources. FCP cannot state with certitude that children who did not appear to be severely distressed when they were referred for treatment and did not experience any of the conditions that are associated with heightened distress may not manifest difficulties later. However, knowledge about these factors that are likely to increase short-term emotional trauma may help a clinician decide between a brief, supportive intervention and longer-term treatment, when the sexual abuse is first disclosed. In this way, the emotional distress associated with sexual abuse may be effectively reduced or eliminated altogether.

NOTE

1. Although theoretically large enough, the statistical requirement that a subject be included in the analysis only if he or she had complete data on all variables, effectively reduced the sample size to make such analyses inappropriate. See discussion of missing data in Chapter 2.

S I X

The Myth of the Mother as "Accomplice" to Child Sexual Abuse

Coauthored with
PATRICIA SALT, MARGARET MYER,
LAURA COLEMAN, and MARIA SAUZIER

Historically, many of the theories about the causes and effects of sexual abuse have focused on the culpability or collusiveness of the victim's mother in permitting the abuse to occur. The clinical literature on incestuous families is replete with examples of the ways in which mothers consciously or unconsciously encourage incestuous relationships between father and child or, at the very least, fail to intercede once they become aware of the sexual activity (Kempe, 1978; Kaufman, Peck, & Taguiri, 1954; Justice & Justice, 1979; Lustig et al. 1966; Peters, 1976; Sarles, 1975). Although far less discussion has centered around the role of mothers in nonincestuous sexual abuse, some investigators have reported that poor mother-daughter relationships (e.g., Finkelhor, 1979) may increase a child's vulnerability to all types of sexual abuse. Some authors have argued that laying the blame on the mother is merely an outgrowth of misogynistic cultural attitudes (McIntyre, 1981). However, the bulk of the literature on incestuous families has been focused on shortcomings in the mother, and as Dietz and Craft (1980) have demonstrated, many protective service workers who treat such families still maintain this belief (see Herman, 1981; Ward, 1985).

The objective of this chapter is to examine the reactions by mothers of sexually abused victims and to explore the reasons why mothers respond in varied ways to the disclosure of the sexual abuse. Throughout this chapter, consideration is given as to whether the theories and research on the reactions of mothers to incest victims are appropriate for understanding the reactions of mothers to other types of child sexual abuse.

Previous Research: An Overview

The prevailing point of view in the literature is that mothers of incest victims typically respond poorly when confronted with allegations that their children are being abused. Reports indicate that often mothers do not take appropriate actions to stop the sexual activity (e.g., Browning & Boatman, 1977; Weinberg, 1955). Meiselman (1978) reports that even when a mother believes her child's report, she may make only feeble efforts to prevent further occurrences of abuse; for example, she may simply avoid leaving the offender and child alone together. In some cases, mothers persist in denying that the sexual abuse has occurred (e.g., Anderson & Shafer, 1979). This denial has been attributed to fear of public humiliation if the abuse is disclosed or to anxieties about the disruption it may cause in the home (Forward & Buck, 1978; Kempe, 1978). Other researchers suggest that the mother may feel torn between assisting her child and protecting her spouse (Burgess, 1978) or that she may fear that acknowledging the incest will lead to divorce and loss of financial support (Forward & Buck, 1978; Meiselman, 1978). In some situations the mother may even fear retaliation from a violent spouse (Browning & Boatman, 1977; Dietz & Craft, 1980).

Some authors report that mothers become angry with the child and blame the child for the abuse (Brooks, 1982; Lustig et al., 1966;

Tormes, 1972), and that this anger may be interpreted as evidence of the mother's wish for the incest to continue in order not to have to deal with her husband's sexual advances (e.g., Kaufman et al., 1954). A more benign interpretation of this anger is that the mother blames the child as an alternative to self-recrimination (Machotka et al., 1966).

There is little in the literature to suggest that mothers respond assertively and empathically to their sexually abused children. Often they are seen as colluding with the offender (Kempe, 1978; Peters, 1976). Indeed, Kempe (1978) contends that "stories by mothers that they could not be more surprised can generally be discounted; we have simply not seen an innocent mother in cases of longstanding incest." More sympathetic authors view these women as passive victims of a patriarchal society, unable to protect either themselves or their children (Meiselman, 1978; Herman & Hirschman, 1981).

Several explanations have been proposed to account for those mothers who do not respond to sexual abuse in a supportive fashion. The primary thesis holds that mothers in incestuous families have fundamental personality problems, which are viewed as outgrowths of deficiencies in caretaking that began during their own youth. Because of their stressful histories and subsequent problems as adults, these mothers develop poor relationships with both their spouses and their children. The consequence is that the mother extricates herself from her role as mother and wife by offering her daughter to her spouse as a sexual "substitute."

Numerous authors have suggested that mothers of incest victims may suffer from hostile, rejecting relationships with their own parents, especially their mothers (Anderson & Shafer, 1979; Brooks, 1982; Lustig et al., 1966; Maisch, 1972). In many cases the mother herself may have been a victim of sexual abuse (Meiselman, 1978). The theory is that this absence of a secure relationship with a caretaker leaves the mother with many ungratified emotional needs and a poor self-concept (Lustig et al., 1966; Goodwin, McCarthy, & DiVasto, 1981; Maisch, 1972).

Hence as adults these women have serious emotional limitations. They are viewed as immature and unable to take responsibility for their actions (Connell, 1978; Kaufman et al., 1954). The typical character style has been described as passive, dependent, and chronically depressed (Browning & Boatman, 1977; Brooks, 1982; Justice & Justice, 1979; Cormier, Kennedy, & Sangowicz, 1962; Pittman, 1977; Sarles, 1975). Some researchers suggest that these women have little capacity to meet the emotional needs of others, and that some may gravitate toward masochistic relationships, choosing aggressive or exploitative mates (Dietz & Craft, 1980; Meiselman, 1978; Tormes, 1972). Even when a woman is not the victim of a violent husband, she may find the demands of her marriage, particularly the sexual relationship, overwhelming or unpleasant (Cormier et al., 1962; Maisch, 1972; Weiner, 1962).

One result is that such women may turn to their children for nurturance. The mother may develop a hostile, dependent relationship with her daughter, replicating the way she interacted with her own mother. She begins to rely upon her daughter to fulfill her needs and assume the responsibilities she finds burdensome. Eventually, the roles are reversed: The daughter becomes the "little woman" in the household and takes on her mother's duties (Brooks, 1982; Browning & Boatman, 1977; Lustig et al., 1966; Kaufman et al., 1954; Justice & Justice, 1979). Ultimately, the child assumes the role of sexual partner with the father (Brooks, 1982; Browning & Boatman, 1977; Lustig et al., 1966).

The image of mothers of incest victims presented in the clinical literature, from the 1950s to the present, is remarkably consistent and uniformly negative. There has been little effort to differentiate subsets of mothers who deviate from the composite image summarized above. Furthermore, there is little data about the ways in which mothers of children who suffer sexual victimization, other than father-daughter incest, differ from this stereotype (Conte, 1982; Faller, 1988).

The FCP experience with mothers of sexual abuse victims suggests that their responses to the sexual abuse and their own psychological characteristics are far more diverse than previous reports have indicated. Because of this, a systematic evaluation of the mothers of the victimized children was undertaken at the time the families entered treatment. This evaluation was designed to assess the extent to which the sample of mothers fit the stereotypic pattern described in the previous literature with respect to: (1) their responses to the sexual abuse; (2) their own psychological development and personality characteristics; and (3) their general relationships with the victimized child. Additionally, FCP examined the extent to which the mother's own history, personality patterns, and attitudes toward the child did, in fact, determine her response to the sexual abuse.

FCP RESEARCH PROCEDURES

Data were drawn from the self-reports of the mothers and the evaluations of the clinicians working with them. Their responses to the sexual abuse were evaluated with two sets of items developed by the Children's Hospital Medical Center (Washington, D.C.) and the URSA Institute. Mothers' personality characteristics were measured with a standardized self-report (Millon Clinical Multiaxial Inventory). FCP also developed a series of questions to gauge the pervasive attitudes toward the victimized children (Parents' Perception of the Child); a further questionnaire was used to gather historical data about the mother's relationship with both her spouse and her parents. The dimensions measured by these instruments are discussed below.

In contrasting the data for mothers who completed the major research measures with those who did not, it was found that the sample of mothers who completed the research measures may not be completely representative of all the cases seen in the clinic. Thus, little data was available on those mothers who were not living with the child at the time treatment began. When a child had been placed in a foster home or an institution, the mother sometimes ceased to play an active role in the child's life, and it is likely that these mothers were excluded from the study. Those mothers who were attempting to regain custody of their children were more likely to participate in the program.

The completion of self-report measures was also influenced by sociological characteristics. Nonwhite mothers were systematically less likely than white mothers to complete self-report measures (e.g., Millon Clinical Multiaxial Inventory). There are indications as well that social class influenced research compliance, with middle-class mothers consistently more likely to complete all of the self-report instruments compared to those in the lowest class. Mothers of children who were first abused during adolescence were also less likely to complete the research measures describing their own personalities. These differences must be kept in mind when interpreting data about mothers' personality characteristics. It is possible that FCP data on psychopathology or self-esteem of the mothers may be influenced by the absence of some poorer, minority mothers.

Overall, however, the absence of any systematic relationship between the type of sexual abuse the child experienced and the availability of information about his or her mother suggests that the data collected were representative of mothers throughout the range of child sexual abuse cases. These data provided FCP with the means to test the hypothesis that mothers typically respond to sexual abuse of their children with inappropriate behavior. (Tables of data analyses are included in Appendix C.)

MATERNAL RESPONSE TO CHILD SEXUAL ABUSE

Researchers have reported a number of common responses to sexual abuse. For example, some suggest that mothers may deny that the abuse is real and fail to take action to put a stop to it; or they may become angry with the victimized child and blame the child for the abuse. To determine how frequently such negative reactions occurred, FCP clinicians rated the attitudes and behavior of each mother at the commencement of treatment. Clinicians' ratings, based on the mother's interview behavior, rather than the mother's self-reports, were used to reduce the extent to which socially desirable answers were automatically offered. From these ratings, six scales were developed: three to assess mothers' *actions* when the sexual abuse was revealed, and three to gauge mothers' *attitudes* toward the child.

The actions of the mothers fell into three major categories: (1) reassuring and protecting the child; (2) scolding or punishing the child; and (3) removing the offender from the home. As illustrated in Table 6.1, more than 80% of the mothers took some form of action to protect the child, ranging from talking to the child about the abuse to preventing the offender from coming into contact with the child. Only 18% failed to take any protective action. In addition, most of the mothers (70%) did not resort to punishing the child. Taking action to remove the offender from the home was, of course, contingent upon whether the offender lived in the child's home and if he refused to leave of his own accord. Therefore, in only 37% of cases was this option possible. In situations where it was possible for a mother to demand that the offender leave, only 22% took such actions. Of course, it is impossible to determine whether removal of the offender was necessary to prevent further abuse. In some cases, mothers may have correctly determined that the child could be protected without removing the offender.

Attitudes toward the sexual abuse showed somewhat similar trends. The emotional reactions of the mother were categorized as: (1) concern for the child's well-being, including absence of protectiveness toward the offender; (2) preoccupation with the effects of the abuse on herself, including self-pity; and (3) anger toward the child. The majority of mothers (90%) demonstrated at least a moderate degree of concern for the child. On the other hand, a relatively large number (45%) were either moderately or strongly preoccupied with the effects of the abuse on themselves. The majority (77%) expressed no hostility or anger toward the victimized child.

Not surprisingly, actions that mothers took in response to the abuse were linked strongly with their emotions. Those mothers who were more concerned about the child were also more likely to take protective action. Similarly, mothers who were angry were more likely to punish the child. However, the extent to which mothers expressed concerns about the effect of the abuse on themselves did not seem to be related to their actions. Indeed, there was some tendency for mothers who expressed concern about their child to manifest similar preoccupations with themselves.

These findings contrast sharply with the overwhelmingly pessimistic view of mothers of sexual abuse victims reported in the previous literature. In fact, the majority of mothers responded

Table 6.1. Mothers' Responses to the Sexual Abuse

Actions[1]		
Protected the child	Not at all	18%
	Some	38%
	Consistently	44%
Punished the child	Not at all	70%
	Some	15%
	Consistently	15%
Removed the offender	No	29%
	Yes	8%
	Not applicable	63%
Attitudes[2]		
Concern for child	Not at all	0%
	Slight	10%
	Moderate	37%
	Strong	53%
Concern for self	Not at all	20%
	Slight	36%
	Moderate	35%
	Strong	10%
Anger toward child	Not at all	77%
	Slight	11%
	Moderate	10%
	Strong	2%

1. Categories represent: all no's on scale items (not at all); mixture of yes and no responses (some); all yes responses (consistently)
2. Categories based on a scale of 1 (not at all) to 4 (a great deal). Average scores: 1.0 = not at all; > 1.0, ≤ 2.0 = slight; > 2.0, ≤ 3.0 = moderate; > 3.0 = strong.

to the revelation of sexual abuse in a reasonably appropriate manner. They expressed concern about the child's welfare and took appropriate steps to protect the child. The majority were *not* angry or punitive. Nevertheless, some of the mothers did fit the negative stereotype described in the literature. Nearly a third of the mothers (30%) were somewhat punitive and 23% expressed some degree of anger (see Table 6.1). Thus, it became important to determine what factors influenced whether a mother would react to her child's sexual victimization with positive caring as opposed to anger and rejection. Previous literature has indicated that mothers' poor responses to sexual victimization of their children can be linked to: (1) their own relationship with the offender; (2) the history of their relationship with parents and subsequent personality development; and (3) their general relationship with the victimized child. Therefore, the extent to which each of these factors helped to explain mothers' reactions to the sexual abuse was assessed.[1]

Impact of Mother's Relationship
with Offender on Response

Much of the previous literature based on cases of incest suggests that mothers who respond unsupportively do so because they feel a greater allegiance to their spouses than to their children. Therefore, one would anticipate that negative reactions to the child by the mother would be less common when the child had been abused by someone outside the family.

Data from the present study indicate that mothers' attitudes and actions were shaped by their relationships with offenders (data in Appendix C). However, there was no simple dichotomy between incest and nonincest. Mothers were least protective and most angry and punitive toward the child when the abuser was not the natural father, but a stepfather or boyfriend. Perhaps in these cases mothers were torn more acutely between allying with their men versus their children. For some women the new husbands or boyfriends may have offered emotional or financial security that was absent when the women were living alone or in relationships with the children's natural fathers. The revelation of the abuse may have created a crisis for the mothers as to what appropriate action they should take. Some mothers may have resolved this conflict by blaming the child. For a mother to believe that this man had abused her child would present a serious threat to the mother's relationship. For others, the allegation of sexual abuse made by their children may actually have represented a major obstacle in preventing them from starting a new life with a new partner.

Similar conflicts of allegiance in families in which the natural father was the offender were anticipated, but for the most part were not observed. Mothers tended to do less to protect the child when the natural father, rather than another relative or an outsider, had abused the child. Perhaps it was especially difficult for them to imagine that a natural father would actually harm his child. However, mothers of children abused by their natural fathers also showed the *least* tendency to be angry or punitive toward the child (see Appendix C). Perhaps this lack of anger toward the child can be explained, in part, by the fact that 45% of the cases of incest with natural fathers did not occur in intact families. These mothers would have little reason to ally with their estranged husbands after their children had been victimized by them. Furthermore, a number of cases of sexual abuse that began when both parents were living together were not revealed until after a divorce or separation. In fact, in some of the cases, the allegations of sexual abuse were initially raised in the context of divorce or custody hearings, and in some cases raised questions about the motives of the parent making the allegations (Corwin, Berliner, Goodman, Goodwin, & White, 1987; Green, 1986).

The idea that mothers who reported better relationships with their partners would feel more conflicts of allegiance when their husbands or lovers were accused of sexual abuse was also supported by the data. Among those cases in which the abuser was a father-figure or natural father, mothers were more likely to express concern about the impact of the abuse on the child and on themselves if they had a poor relationship with their spouse. In contrast, mothers were more likely to be angry with the child because of the abuse if they had a more satisfying marital relationship. However, there was no indication that incest mothers as a group had poorer relationships with their spouses than other mothers in the sample.

These results support the notion that mothers who feel conflicts in allegiance between the child who has been sexually abused and the partner who committed the abuse may resolve their conflict by blaming the child for the abuse. However, this phenomenon was certainly not ubiquitous in incest families.

Clinical evaluation of those mothers whose children were victims of incest indicated four different types of response to the abuse. The first group responded decisively and without ambivalence to protect their children. These mothers directed their anger toward the offender, and in no way blamed the child for the abuse. Further, they took protective actions without being pressured by authorities. A second group were more conflicted in their allegiances. These mothers felt empathy for both their children and their spouses and often had difficulty taking strong enough action to protect the victim without the intervention of protective services. A third group was immobilized by the disclosure of the abuse. Not only did they deny the occurrence or significance of the abuse, but they showed only moderate concern for their children. They did not, however, blame the child for the abuse. The last group of mothers clearly rejected their children. In addition to siding with their mates, they took no action to protect the child.

Although in-depth clinical evaluation of the nonincest mother was not attempted, the overall data on responses suggest that these women may fall into similar categories. Thus, it is important to determine what characteristics of the mother may have led her to respond more or less supportively.

Effect of Personality on
Response by Mother

A primary theory about mothers of sexually abused children holds that they are passive, dependent women with poor self-esteem. Furthermore, these personality characteristics are presumed to be the consequence of a stressful childhood, marked by cold, distant relationships with parents and sometimes a history of sexual abuse.

To assess the validity of this description, the extent to which the mothers in this sample displayed the characteristic personality patterns described in the literature—passivity, emotional inhibition, poor interpersonal relations—was measured. To gain an understanding of the different types of personality patterns mothers displayed, their responses to the Millon Clinical Multiaxial Inventory were statistically analyzed. These analyses yielded scales that measured the typical configuration of characteristics that were evident in subgroups of mothers, as well as the extent to which each mother displayed that pattern of problems (see Appendix C). Thus, it was possible to determine whether mothers displayed other types of personalities different from the passive, compliant type described in the literature, as well as the proportion of mothers who showed evidence of having the problems described in each pattern.

General personality styles or types of emotional problems were described by five scales developed from the Millon Clinical Multiaxial Inventory. As noted in Table 6.2, pathology on these scales ranged from no evidence of the problem, a minor degree of difficulty that would not necessarily have required psychiatric intervention, to difficulties serious enough to merit treatment.

The personality dimensions of the mothers include the passive, submissive pattern described in the literature. Mothers with high scores on the *submission* dimension were compliant and dependent upon others for direction. When they did take action, they were guided by their immediate feelings and often were unable to think through their decisions systematically. While 21% of the mothers displayed major problems in this area, few (12%) were completely asymptomatic. This result does lend some support to the diagnostic picture of mothers of sexual abuse victims depicted in the literature.

However, submission was not the only personality pattern found in the sample. Four other typical patterns of emotional dysfunction were also observed among the mothers. First, *emotional lability* was characterized by extreme mood swings, ranging from depression to excitement. Mothers high in emotional lability were often described by friends or family as being "high strung" or moody. These mothers were prone to misusing alcohol. In all, 25% of the mothers exhibited serious problems with emotional lability. Second, *socially withdrawn* characterized mothers who were disinterested in social interactions with others. They represented the type of

The Myth of Mother as "Accomplice"

Table 6.2. Mothers' Personality Problems

| | Degree of Problems[1] | | |
Scales	No Symptoms	Minor Symptoms	Major Symptoms
Submission	12%	67%	21%
Emotional Lability	23%	48%	25%
Social Withdrawal	19%	62%	19%
Reality Distortion	26%	61%	13%
Negativism	54%	31%	15%

1. Scores on the Millon Clinical Multiaxial Inventory were categorized: 0–45 = no symptoms; 45 to 75 = minor symptoms; 75 to 120 = major symptoms.

individual who actively avoids initiating social relationships. In all, 19% of the mothers of sexually abused children had serious problems in this area. The type of social ineptness or disinterest measured by this scale appears to fit with the image of incest families as psychologically isolated from others. Third, *reality distortion* was characteristic of women who had an unrealistic view of the world, in particular, of women who were persistently suspicious of the motives of others. Mothers with such problems occasionally also abused drugs. Serious problems in this area were least common. However, 13% of the mothers did manifest severe examples of these difficulties. The fourth pattern was *negativism*, or opposition to conventional norms. Mothers displaying this personality style were unlikely to be excessively conformist. Rather, they tended to act on their impulses, with some abusing drugs. Overall, relatively few mothers exhibited serious problems in this area (15%), and more than half (54%) showed no evidence of a negativistic style.

The data on pathological personality characteristics suggest that the majority of mothers did not have serious emotional problems that would immediately identify them as candidates for psychiatric treatment. In fact, only 18% had received prior psychiatric care. A majority of mothers did exhibit some signs of problems in all areas except negativistic, nonconforming behavior. While some degree of difficulty with passivity and submission was more common (88%) than any other problem, there was little strong evidence to support the notion that this style is either universal or a source of major emotional dysfunction in these mothers. More importantly, there was no evidence indicating that any of these behavior patterns were more prevalent in incest mothers. Clinical diagnosis of the incest mothers indicated that they present a wide spectrum of problems and that diagnostic category was unrelated to the adequacy of the mothers' responses to the victimized children.

Data on the mothers' history of relationships do support the notion that many of these women had some factors in their background that may have predisposed them to respond inappropriately to their child's sexual abuse. Nearly half the mothers (45%) described the relationships with their own mothers as indifferent to overtly hostile, and 39% described their relationships with their fathers in the same terms. More than a third (34%) had been physically abused or neglected as children, and 41% had been sexually abused (see Goodwin et al., 1981). In adulthood, 39% had been physically abused by their husbands or lovers. Comparison of these figures with available data on rates of sexual and physical abuse suggests that there is reason to believe that this sample of women did have especially traumatic childhood experiences. For instance, Finkelhor found that 19% of a large sample of women had been sexually abused as children, and the National Study of the Incidence and Severity of Child Abuse and Neglect (National Center for Child Abuse and Neglect, 1981) estimated that only 10.5 children in a thousand were maltreated each year. However, it is noteworthy that mothers in father-child incest cases were no more likely to report poor parental relations or a history of physical or sexual abuse than any of the other mothers in the sample. Indeed, there was a slight tendency for mothers of children who had been abused by someone outside the family to report the worst relationships with their own mothers. There was also a slightly lower incidence of physical abuse during childhood for mothers whose children were abused by their natural fathers.

Examination of the clinical records of incest mothers provides some insight into this absence of an overall difference between incest and nonincest mothers. Poor relationships with their own mothers or the absence of any significant mother-figure were prevalent among those mothers who took no action or rejected their children, but not among the more protective mothers. The more important question, however, is whether the presence of emotional difficulties or a history of emotional deprivation necessarily predisposes these women to respond unsupportively when their children report sexual abuse. The data (Appendix C) suggest that one type of personality difficulty does consistently influence mothers' reactions. Those mothers who were especially emotionally labile were more likely to be concerned about the effect of the abuse on themselves and to be more angry with the child. Ironically, more labile mothers were also more likely to take action to protect the child. These findings begin to make more sense if one considers the difficulties these mothers have in modulating their feelings. They may feel overwhelmed by the revelation of the abuse. Unsure of whom to blame and whom to comfort, they begin to behave somewhat erratically. They take action to protect the child, but simultaneously blame the child for "creating the whole mess." The end result is a disruption of the mother's fragile equilibrium. Only one other personality characteristic influenced the reactions of the mothers to the abuse—more socially withdrawn mothers were more likely to be angry with their children.

There was also some evidence that a history of a poor relationship between the mother and either of her parents impacted the mother's capacity to express concern for her sexually abused child (Appendix C). Mothers who had a poor relationship with their fathers were also less capable of taking protective action. However, there was no indication that those mothers who had been sexually abused themselves responded any differently to their child's abuse than mothers who had not been abused. Thus, we might speculate that the mothers who had difficulty expressing concern or taking action in response to the abuse may have been hampered by an absence of positive role models for parenting in their own childhood. However, there is little reason to believe that these same mothers were dealing with particular issues of sexuality or sexual exploitation from their own childhood.

*Impact of Mothers' Relationship
to the Child on Response
by Mother*

Many authors suggest that as a corollary to their emotional difficulties mothers of sexually abused children develop distorted relationships with their children. It is believed that these mothers are not only unable to offer nurturance, but instead expect to be cared for by the child. To test whether the mothers in FCP did indeed evidence problems in interacting with their victimized children (presumably predating the revelation of the sexual abuse), ratings of the mother's relationship with the child were determined. These ratings were compiled into four scales. *Caring* signified that the mother's general relationship with the child was characterized by affection and concern. *Depending* described maternal intrusiveness and reliance upon the child as a source of support. This scale captured, in part, the tendency described in previous reports for mothers to delegate their own wifely or caretaking responsibilities to the victimized child. The third scale, *burdened*, gauged a lack of emotional availability on the mother's part, which has been hypothesized as a feature of incest mothers. Mothers who feel overburdened by their child's needs may have difficulty expressing affection or pride in the child. The *hostile* scale measured pervasive anger toward the child and the perception that the child was bad.

The pattern of mothers' general relationships shown in Table 6.3 indicates that the overwhelming majority of mothers (97%) had moderate to high nurturing attitudes toward the victimized child, while relatively few were obviously hostile toward that child (8%). More subtle indicators of difficulties in the mother-child relationship were, however, evident. More than 2 out of every 5 mothers (43%) showed some tendency to rely upon the child to gratify their own needs, while 41% felt overburdened by their children's emotional demands.

Not surprisingly, the quality of the mother's relationship with the victimized child was also influenced by her relations with her own parents (data in Appendix C). Mothers who had poor relationships with their own mothers were especially likely to feel

Table 6.3. Mothers' General Relationship with the Victimized Child

Caring	low	3%
	moderate	44%
	high	53%
Depending	low	57%
	moderate	37%
	high	6%
Burdened	low	57%
	moderate	37%
	high	4%
Hostile	low	53%
	moderate	39%
	high	8%

Note: Scores were based on a scale of 1–5: 1–1.99 = low; 2.0–3.99 = moderate; 4.0–5.0 = high.

dependent upon the child, while a poor relationship with her father increased the likelihood that the mother would feel overburdened by her child's needs. Contrary to previous reports, neither dependence upon the child, nor lack of emotional availability was more common in mothers of incest victims. However, findings on the relationship between types of incestuous abuse and generally caring or hostile mother/child relationships paralleled findings about mothers' reactions to the abuse. Mothers whose children had been victimized by their current lovers or husbands (i.e., not the child's natural father) generally had less caring and more hostile relationships with their children than mothers whose children were victimized by someone outside the family.

The relationship between mothers' typical relationships with their children and the ways in which they responded to the abuse were affirmed by analyses of the entire sample (data in Appendix C). Mothers who usually had a caring relationship with the child were likely to be concerned and to behave protectively when they heard about the abuse and were not likely to be angry or punitive. The relationship between generally hostile attitudes toward the child and responses to the sexual abuse nearly mirrored this image. Mothers who were usually hostile were especially likely to be angry and punitive in response to the sexual abuse and unlikely to be concerned or protective. Similarly, mothers who tended to be overburdened by their children's needs were especially likely to respond to the abuse angrily and unlikely to be supportive.

In contrast, a mother's dependency upon a child to gratify her needs was not related to either appropriate or inappropriate actions in response to the abuse. Dependent mothers were especially likely to express concerns about the impact of the sexual abuse on themselves. Generally caring mothers, however, also showed this tendency. As already noted, a mother's tendency to focus upon her own distress about the abuse does not necessarily mean that she is unable to respond appropriately to her child. One might expect, however, important qualitative differences between the self-concerns expressed by caring mothers and those who have some expectation that their children should take care of them. Indeed, this distinction might provide a clue for explaining why some mothers resolve their ambivalence between a spouse and the child by mobilizing to protect the child, while others feel too needy and dependent to relinquish their relationships with the men who offer them some measure of security.

Extrafamilial Influences and
Response by Mother

There has been little discussion in the literature about factors other than the mother's emotional problems that might account for her response to her child's sexual victimization. To deal with this issue, FCP explored whether there were any broad sociocultural factors that influenced the type of response, and whether the response was related to any characteristics of the abuse, aside from whether or not it was incestuous.

The data (see Appendix C) indicate that the mothers' broader cultural background and expectations may have had some effect on their reactions. Mothers from lower social classes tended to be less protective of their children, more punitive, and less concerned for the child's welfare. Nonwhite mothers were more likely than white mothers to punish or blame the child for the abuse. These differences may be explained in part by the heightened stresses in the lives of poor families. When parents must struggle to ensure that their families have appropriate food and housing, they may be too emotionally overburdened to provide much support to the victimized child. Also, the response may reflect underlying attitudes toward childrearing in certain subcultures. Some mothers may be more inclined to believe that their children were victimized because the child misbehaved in some way, thereby provoking the attack. Conversely, these mothers may view the sexual abuse as just another instance of the child causing trouble or embarrassment for the family.

Negative responses on the part of the mother may also be linked to their expectations about sexual behavior. Although one would expect that more educated, affluent parents might be less likely to attribute responsibility for the sexual abuse to the child, there was evidence that the whole sample of mothers may have had expectations that some children are less culpable than others. For example, mothers were more protective and less punitive when the victimized child was a son rather than a daughter. Further, mothers expressed greater concern and protective behavior the younger the victimized child, while being more angry and punitive with older children. These findings support the premise that some parents may hold the child, especially an older girl, as being responsible for initiating the sexual activity. Thus, a child's sense of guilt about not being able to stop an offender may be reinforced by overt or covert messages from the parent that the child should have been able to prevent the abuse. That parents may convey some sense that the child should have stopped the sexual activity is also supported by the finding that mothers were most concerned and protective in cases in which the child did not delay in disclosing the sexual abuse.

CONCLUSIONS

The depiction of mothers of sexual abuse victims in the previous literature emphasizes that the inadequacies of many mothers presumably allow the sexual abuse to begin; that once begun, these inadequacies prevent the mothers from taking any definitive action to either stop the abuse or to protect the child when the abuse has been openly revealed. The findings in the present study clearly challenge the universality of this image of mothers as willing accomplices in incest or other types of sexual abuse (see also Faller, 1988). First of all, mothers respond to the sexual abuse of their children in a variety of ways. Although some do fit the stereotype and do respond to the revelation of sexual abuse by blaming the child or refusing to believe the allegations, many more are able to mobilize their energies to ensure that the child will no longer be victimized and to support the child during the difficult process of resolving the sexual abuse situation. Even when faced with the dilemma of choosing between a partner whom they rely upon for emotional and financial support and the child who has accused this partner of sexual abuse, some risk losing an important relationship in order to attend to the child's needs.

The current findings suggest that some of the variability in a mother's responses to sexual abuse is influenced by the quality of her relationships, both with her own parents and with the child. Mothers who report a poorer history of emotional nurturance in their own childhood are less able to develop nurturing relationships with their children. This phenomenon is not unique to sexual abuse, it is a widely recognized issue in child psychiatry (Fraiberg, 1975). When a mother feels that she must get emotional support from her child, it is difficult for her to respond empathically to that child in a crisis. The mother's own needs are so great that she does not have the psychic resources to attend to the needs of anyone else. However, a noteworthy finding is that such an inability to empathize with the child is found in both incest and nonincest mothers. Thus, the notion that a history of poor parenting (possibly compounded by sexual abuse) predisposes a woman to enter into a marital relationship with a man who will sexually abuse her children is not supported. The finding by FCP that "incest" mothers are not fundamentally different from mothers of other sexual abuse victims presents a striking parallel to recent research showing the distinction between perpetrators of incest and extrafamilial abuse to be less precise than that previously portrayed. Many incest fathers also victimize other children. Perhaps mothers who have less capacity to nurture their children increase the chances that their children will be victimized in some way. They may be less aware of cues that the child might be in danger and less diligent in supervising their children. However, there is no reason to believe that the primary reason children are sexually abused is because they have inadequate mothers or that all mothers of incest victims are inadequate.

The data support the notion that mothers in father-child incest cases have greater difficulty empathizing with the child when they have a good relationship with the spouse who is accused of the abuse. When a mother must make a choice between two beloved people in her life, it is understandable that there will be some internal conflict. However, clinical observations by FCP indicate that numerous mothers have the ability to appropriately protect their children, despite their attachment to the offender.

In interpreting the current research findings, it is important to emphasize that FCP was measuring the responses of the mothers to the sexual abuse at the time they first entered treatment. Further clinical observations suggest that these initial reactions do not necessarily predict the eventual capacity of the mothers to take the actions needed to protect their children. The evolution of the responses (by the mothers) to the disclosure of sexual abuse may be likened to the grieving process, in which there is a passage from denial through anger and depression before the traumatizing reality can be accepted (Kubler-Ross, 1969). When a mother discovers that her child has been sexually abused, her initial reaction is often shock and denial. Furthermore, when the alleged offender is someone close, the mother may find it difficult to believe that this person could have done such a thing. For some mothers, the denial is very short-lived; within moments they accept the unpleasant reality and mobilize themselves to respond. For others, refusing to believe that the abuse could have taken place may persist for a longer time. These mothers may need considerable therapeutic intervention before they can accept their child's allegations. Some mothers are never able to acknowledge the sexual abuse, and resist all efforts at having them engage in treatment.

Once mothers accept the reality of the sexual abuse, they often experience a period of guilt and self-recrimination. Many berate themselves for not having seen clues that the abuse had been going on or for not having taken action when they first suspected that something might be amiss. There may then be a period of anger toward the offender and an ensuing depression as they contemplate the losses and disruptions in their lives. Finally, the acceptance that the sexual abuse has taken place allows the mother to begin working toward restoring equilibrium within the family unit.

Of course, not all mothers are able to proceed through the entire process. As already noted, some never break through their denial. Others may become so mired in depression and self-pity that they are unable to help their children or themselves get beyond the abuse. Treatment may play an important role in developing the mother's capacity to respond appropriately to her victimized child. Observation of these mothers in treatment suggests that there are some characteristics that are useful in predicting which mothers will be best able to make use of clinical services. Mothers who initially appear to be psychologically healthier may get past the initial denial more quickly. Also, mothers who are actively angry about the abuse and angry with the offender are more likely to become engaged in therapy. The greater the mother's initial capacity to feel empathy for the child, the more likely she is to profit from treatment.

The notion that mothers are the true culprits when their children are sexually abused is widespread. Unfortunately, this attitude may lead to inappropriate and harmful interventions when sexual abuse is revealed. Mothers who show the slightest tendency to deny the allegations may be accused of collusion. In some cases, agencies may act precipitously to remove victimized children from the mother's care. The findings by FCP suggest that a more thorough evaluation of the mother's capacity to work through the trauma of discovering that her child has been sexually abused is necessary. Only after a complete evaluation is it possible to make sound judgments about whether a mother will be able to provide her child with sufficient support and protection to prevent any further sexual abuse from occurring.

NOTE

1. Since removal of the offender was only relevant for a small subsample of cases, this dimension of mothers' responses to the abuse was not included in further analyses.

SEVEN

The Aftermath of Child
Sexual Abuse: 18 Months Later

Coauthored with
MARIA SAUZIER

As the psychiatric, social service, and legal professions have become
sensitized to the prevalence of child sexual victimization, there has
been increased pressure to intervene: to prevent new abuse, to
halt ongoing sexual activity, and to offer services to victimized
children and their families. Knowledge, however, about the long-
term consequences of child sexual abuse and the efficacy of
intervention strategies is limited. As noted in Chapter 5, no
consensus has been reached on whether or not substantial
proportions of these children evidence difficulties in later life
(Browne & Finkelhor, 1986). The results from the present study
support the idea that children who have been recently abused seem
to manifest more emotional and behavioral problems than their
peers in the general population (Conte & Schuerman, 1987; Kiser
et al., 1988; Murphy et al., 1988; Sirles et al., 1989). Yet, it is equally
evident that not all of the sexually victimized children were seriously
disturbed; some had no clinical symptoms.

The disturbance or lack of disturbance that children exhibit when
sexual victimization is initially revealed may not necessarily reflect

their eventual strategy for coping with the sexual experiences. As discussed in the conceptual framework used to understand the sources of trauma in child sexual abuse (Chapter 2), some of the distress a child displays when first entering treatment may be evoked by the turmoil that surrounds the disclosure of the abuse. When parents become anxious, or when outside agencies such as the police or protective services intervene, the child is likely to become upset. Once the crisis of disclosure has been resolved, either by restoring calm in an agitated family, changing the family constellation to reduce the threat of further sexual abuse, or moving the child to a more stable, protective environment, some of the stress evoked by the exposure of the sexual abuse may be reduced. Other children may appear to have few symptoms of emotional distress when they initially enter treatment because they have not yet grasped the full significance of their victimization. As noted in Chapter 5, this is especially likely when the child is too young or too intellectually limited to understand the social reprobation associated with adult-child sexual contact. In some of these cases, children who initially appear unharmed may later experience shame or guilt about their experience. Thus, it is unclear whether the level of distress observed by FCP in recently victimized children is predictive of their eventual adaptation.

There is considerable agreement that the way in which the sexual abuse is handled when it is first revealed has an important impact upon the child's eventual adjustment. Few would dispute that intervention carries the potential for harm as well as help. However, distinguishing interventions that cause harm from those that enhance the prospect of the child's emerging from abusive experience without sustaining long-term emotional scars is difficult. The FCP was established with the presumption that brief psychotherapeutic treatment would reduce some of the distress associated with the sexual abuse. While numerous service providers and researchers concur in the belief that counseling the victimized child and his or her family reduces distress (Burgess, Holmstrom, & McCausland, 1978; Sgroi, 1982), Goldstein, Freud and Solnit (1979) contend that the disruption in the child's life occasioned by therapeutic intervention may outweigh the benefits of treatment.

Definitive answers to these issues will require more complex research designs than are now possible in this relatively new field. However, the follow-up data collected from families of sexual abuse victims one to two years after they were referred to the FCP offers some preliminary insights into the range of interventions that families experience after the sexual abuse has been disclosed, as well as changes in emotional distress that occur in these children during this period. The FCP assessment of the victims of sexual abuse when they first entered treatment indicated that the group exhibited more emotional and behavioral problems than children in the general population. Although it is impossible to assess how much of this disturbance was attributable to the sexual abuse itself, FCP presumed that the experience of being victimized and the disruption occasioned by the disclosure of the abuse did heighten the distress of these children. Thus, the following questions were asked at follow-up: (1) Do victimized children show changes in distress after therapy?; (2) To what extent do these changes signify an improvement in the child's psychological functioning?; and (3) Are any of the changes associated with the experiences of the children during their initial FCP treatment or in the follow-up period?

ASSESSMENT AT FOLLOW-UP

Three measures were used to assess the victimized child's emotional and behavioral functioning at follow-up. First, the overall level of psychopathology was gauged by the Severity Level score from the Louisville Behavior Checklist; second, self-esteem was measured by the Piers-Harris and Purdue Self-Concept Scales, and lastly, change in particular symptoms frequently associated with child sexual abuse were assessed with the Child and Adolescent Behavior Checklists developed by the Children's Hospital National Medical Center (Washington, D.C.).

Although many aspects of the child's life may change because of the sexual abuse, this chapter focuses on two major issues—whether the sexual abuse and its revelation lead to disruption and dissolution of the family unit and the extent to which the child received therapeutic intervention.

Overall Pathology

At the conclusion of the follow-up, the sample of victims, as a whole, showed a significant decrease in overall psychopathology and an increase in positive self-esteem. In all, 75% of the youngsters in the 4- to 13-year-old range did not exhibit significant psychopathology when compared with the general population. More individualized assessment of change (see Table 7.1) indicated that the majority of the children showed significant improvements in overall behavioral disturbance and in self-esteem during the follow-up period. Some children did not improve and another group actually exhibited significantly worse problems at follow-up. Thus, although the average amount of change for the entire sample of victims was substantial, considerable variability existed in the outcomes of specific cases. Examination of the relationships between improvement in overall level of emotional distress and demographic characteristics of the child indicated that neither age, sex, race, nor socioeconomic status influenced whether the child improved. Similarly, no significant association can be made between characteristics of the sexual abuse such as duration, degree of violence, relationship with the offender, and the likelihood that a child would show improvement.

Whether the child showed improvement in overall psychopathology was related to the child's initial level of distress upon entering treatment. The results in Table 7.2 suggest that children who were initially asymptomatic were most likely to exhibit increased problems at follow-up. In contrast, those who had been most disturbed initially were most likely to show improvement. To a certain extent these results may reflect a statistical artifact— when individuals with unusually high scores on a measure are retested, their new scores tend to be closer to the average. However, the findings also support the observations that (1) some flagrant disturbances may be related to the stress of revelation and subside

Table 7.1. Change in Emotional Distress of Victim from Intake
to Follow-Up

Measure	Improved	No Change	Worse
Louisville Severity Level (N = 77)	55%	21%	24%
Self-concept (N = 81)	57%	11%	32%

Criteria for improved and worse: change scores greater than 1.95 x standard error of
measurement.

Table 7.2. Relationship Between Initial Severity of Behavior Disturbance
and Improvement: Louisville Behavior Checklist

Initial Severity of Symptoms*	Improved**	% Who Didn't Change	Worsened
No symptoms (N = 34)	35%	35%	30%
Mild symptoms (N = 32)	63%	16%	22%
Severe symptoms (N = 11)	91%	0%	9%

*Criteria for categories: Louisville Severity Level Scores normed for a clinical population.
No symptoms = < 40; mild symptoms = 40 to 55; severe symptoms = > 55.
**Criteria for improved and worsened: change scores greater than and less than
1.95 x standard error of measurement.

relatively quickly, and (2) some children who initially appear
unaffected by the abuse may later be beset with problems.

Common Symptoms

   To gain a better understanding of the specific types of changes
that occurred in this sample of sexually abused children, FCP
examined those individual problems from the Child and Adolescent
Behavior Checklists that were observed most frequently at intake.
For children 12 years old and younger, FCP examined the 12
symptoms that were most often checked at the start of treatment
on the Child Behavior Checklist. These symptoms, listed in Table
7.3, included several that have been consistently associated with

Table 7.3. Child Behavior Checklist—Change, Intake to 18-Month Follow-Up

Symptom	Total % Symptomatic at Intake[1]	% Never Had Symptom	% Improved	Total % Asymptomatic at Follow-Up[2]	% Stayed Symptomatic	% Got Worse	Total % Symptomatic at Follow-Up[3]
Irritability (N = 70)	56	27	27	54	29	17	46
Seeks Attention (N = 71)	60	17	21	38	39	23	62
Keeps Feelings In (N = 72)	50	33	32	65	18	17	35
Fears (N = 72)	56	28	25	53	31	17	47
Sleep Problems (N = 70)	51	43	41	84	10	6	16
Worried, Tense (N = 71)	40	41	27	68	13	20	32
Afraid of Offender (N = 68)	47	46	22	68	25	7	32
Nervous, Jittery (N = 72)	38	50	26	76	11	13	24
Behaving Older Than Age (N = 68)	40	46	13	59	27	15	41
Crying (N = 71)	37	42	24	66	13	21	34
Argues With Parents (N = 71)	42	38	14	52	28	20	48
Argues With Siblings (N = 71)	44	27	11	38	33	29	62

1. Sum of those who later improved and those who stayed symptomatic.
2. Sum of those who never had the symptom and those who improved.
3. Sum of those who stayed symptomatic and those who got worse.

sexual abuse (e.g., fear of the offender, generalized fears, and sleep problems) and others that represent more common childhood problems (e.g., arguing with siblings or parents). Analysis of the pattern of changes in these problems is consistent with the data on overall emotional disturbance. Although the majority of children were no longer symptomatic at the time of follow-up, others apparently developed new symptoms during the follow-up phase that were not evident when they entered treatment.

Examination of individual symptoms indicated that certain signs of acute distress were unlikely to appear later if they were not evident when treatment began. Sleep problems and fear of the offender worsened in less than 10% of the cases. For most symptoms, the overall effect of treatment and the passage of time was to decrease the proportion of children presenting the problem behavior, but rates of improvement were most dramatic for signs of anxiety—sleep problems, worry, nervousness, irritability, and signs of inner tension, such as keeping feelings hidden. In a few areas the group seemed to exhibit more problem behavior than they had at the start of treatment. The rate of fighting with siblings had increased from 44% to 62%, while arguments with parents and seeking extra attention also showed slight increases.

For some of the children, the increased family discord reflected the recriminations and blame-seeking that followed the revelation of intrafamily sexual abuse. In some cases, siblings felt that the victimized child had caused "trouble" in the family. Because the average child in the sample was making the transition from late childhood into early adolescence during the follow-up period, some of the increased argumentativeness that was observed might also have been attributable to a heightened striving to differentiate oneself from one's parents, a natural accompaniment to adolescent development.

Similar analyses of changes in the 13 symptoms most often observed in adolescents at intake into the program are reported in Table 7.4. These data also show a pattern of both improvement and development of new problems during the follow-up period. As was witnessed for the younger children, sleep problems dramatically subsided (from 55% to 17% of the sample). Similarly,

Table 7.4. Adolescent Behavior Checklist—Change Between Intake to 18-Month Follow-Up

Symptom	Total % Symptomatic at Intake[1]	% Never Had Symptom	% Improved	Total % Asymptomatic at Follow-Up[2]	% Stayed Symptomatic	% Got Worse	Total % Symptomatic at Follow-Up[3]
Keeping Feelings In	69	17	10	27	59	14	73
Depression	57	33	37	70	20	10	30
Argues With Parents	66	13	23	36	43	20	63
Argues With Siblings	46	11	7	18	39	43	82
Feels Ugly	50	43	37	80	13	7	20
Confused About Sex	63	30	53	83	10	7	17
Feels Lonely	53	33	43	76	10	13	23
Afraid of Offender	47	33	37	70	10	20	30
Sleep Problems	55	35	48	83	7	10	17
Down on Self	46	47	33	80	13	7	20
Worried, Tense	50	32	36	68	14	18	32
Nervous, Jittery	39	52	36	88	3	10	30
Extra Attention	46	47	33	80	13	7	20

1. Sum of those who later improved and those who stayed symptomatic.
2. Sum of those who never had the symptom and those who improved.
3. Sum of those who stayed symptomatic and those who got worse.

confusion about sexuality, needing extra attention, and self-denigration (e.g., feeling ugly or "down" on oneself) decreased to the extent that only 20% or less of the group showed those problems at follow-up. The finding that arguments with parents showed no improvement and arguments with siblings substantially increased (i.e., from 46% to 80%) parallels the findings noted in the younger children.

One intriguing contrast between symptom changes in the younger children and the adolescents was that the younger children showed a slight increase in attention seeking and a sizable decrease in keeping feelings private, while adolescents manifested nearly opposite effects—substantially decreased need for attention and slightly increased reluctance to disclose feelings. Again, some of these differences might be attributable to normal developmental processes. As they mature, adolescents are more likely to depend less upon parents for attention or counsel. However, the results also raise the question of whether younger and older victims learned somewhat different strategies for maintaining emotional equilibrium while they were in treatment.

Inappropriate Sexual Activity

In addition to the commonly reported symptoms in children and adolescents, a potential problem of sexually abused children has occasioned considerable discussion. Several evaluations of adolescents and adults have indicated that children who are sexually victimized may be revictimized or may later sexually victimize others (e.g., Groth, 1979), while others may become involved in inappropriate activities, such as prostitution (James & Meyerding, 1977; Lloyd, 1976). It is difficult to assess this question less than two years after the child has been victimized. Only limited information on revictimization and sexually inappropriate behavior during the follow-up period exists.

The follow-up interviews revealed a low incidence of reported revictimization. In only five cases did a parent or official custodian of the child report revictimization; in two instances the mothers' fear that their estranged husbands were reabusing the preschool children appeared to be unsubstantiated. In the remaining cases, the preadolescent girls came from extremely disorganized environments and were revictimized by family members. In one case a girl who had been removed from her home because of sexual abuse indicated she was revictimized when she visited with her mother, but no details were available. The other two girls had initially not been removed from their homes because the father-figure who committed the abuse had left. One was revictimized by an older brother and the other was reabused by her mother's boyfriend when the mother allowed him to return.

The latter case involved a 15-year-old girl who had been victimized by her father. She later became sexually involved with the foster-father in the home in which she was placed and fled the state with him. Although the girl's involvement with the older man appeared to be consensual, the activity met the study's criteria for abuse. This case, in particular, points out the difficulty of distinguishing between "revictimization" and "acting out conflicts through sexuality" in those children who have been sexually abused previously.

The extent to which the victimized children (aged 12 and younger) exhibited signs of inappropriate sexual activity was assessed with several questions. The Child Behavior Checklist included two items measuring excessive sexual preoccupation and inappropriate sex play. The data in Table 7.5 indicate little evidence of exacerbation in these problems during the follow-up period. Sexual preoccupation showed a slight overall increase, which may in part reflect that some of the children were nearing adolescence. For instance, one mother complained that her 12-year-old daughter had become "boy-crazy." Overall, however, inappropriate sex-play actually showed some decline.

Data on sexual responses for adolescents yielded somewhat similar results (Table 7.6). Over time, they were less likely to view themselves as sexually promiscuous and were less likely to fear sexual contact with others. The trend appears to be toward a more comfortable integration of their sexuality. There were some exceptions; one adolescent boy who had been sexually abused by

Table 7.5. Percent of Children Age 12 and Younger, with Sexually
Inappropriate Behavior

	N	Sexual Preoccupation %	N	Inappropriate Sex-Play %
At intake	87	21%	94	18%
18 months after FCP	75	31%	72	10%

Table 7.6. Self-Reported Sexual Activity by Adolescents

	N	Feeling Sexually "Too Loose" %	N	Afraid of Sex %
At intake	49	14%	47	40%
18 months after FCP	38	3%	37	24%

his two older brothers was arrested twice for molesting very young children during the follow-up period. Another adolescent boy was placed in a juvenile detention facility, primarily because of his activities as a prostitute. Two of the female victims also had some contact with the police because of allegations of prostitution, but they denied the charges.

EXPERIENCE DURING FOLLOW-UP

Once sexual abuse is disclosed, a number of forces are set into action that may dramatically change the lives of the victimized child and his or her family. Some of the interceding events may diminish the distress a child feels, while others may heighten it. One factor repeatedly discussed in the literature is the disruption of the family that may occur when the sexual abuse is revealed. A second major factor that FCP hypothesized as possibly having an impact upon the child's adjustment is whether or not the child continued to receive treatment services following the crisis intervention process.

Family Disruption

Those who argue that the revelation of sexual abuse may sometimes cause more distress that the abuse itself usually point to the family disruption that results when a variety of agencies intercede to handle the abuse. As noted in Chapter 5, those children who had been removed from their homes because of sexual abuse manifested high levels of emotional distress when they entered treatment. Whether the distress was *caused* by the removal of the child or was one of the reasons why protective service workers decided that placement was necessary could not be distinguished. However, it is important to determine how often family disruption does result from the disclosure of the sexual abuse, and if the children from disrupted families do continue to have more problems.

During the FCP follow-up period, 51% of the children who were evaluated had experienced some change in parenting—a parent left home or returned, a new parent-figure joined the family, or the child was placed in another setting. These changes meant that approximately 18 months after the families entered treatment less than half of the children (46%) were living with the same parents they had lived with when they were sexually abused.

Although the average child experienced one change in family constellation, the range extended to eight changes. It is difficult to imagine that a child who has lived in eight different family settings during less than two years could maintain a sense of continuity or emotional security. Comparison of the types of family patterns at the time the child was abused and at follow-up (Table 7.7) suggests that the major shift was a decrease in two-parent families and an increase in children living away from their natural parents.

Review of the nature of the changes in family patterns during the follow-up (see Table 7.8) also confirmed this impression; most of the changes involved loss of contact with the biological parents.

Table 7.7. Parental Figures in the Home at the Time of the Sexual Abuse, Compared with Follow-Up Period

Parents	Percent at Time of Sex Abuse	Percent at Follow-Up
Two-Parent	43%	30%
Single-Parent	48%	42%
Other Setting*	9%	24%

*Foster care, group home, etc.

Table 7.8. Reasons Why the Family Constellation Changed During the Follow-Up Period

Reason for Change in Family	Percent of Cases[1]
Parent left (N = 139 known cases)	
Natural parent	9%
Surrogate parent	5%
Parent Joined (N = 139 known cases)	
Parent returned	4%
New father joined	6%
Child changed home (N = 143 known cases)	
Placed with other natural parent	7%
Placed with relative	7%
Placed with family friend	6%
Foster home	3%
Group home or institution	13%
Emergency shelter	11%
Detention center	6%
Runaway	1%

1. Percents sum to more than 51% total changed during follow-up because of multiple changes for the same child.

And 39% of the changes signified a child was living away from blood relations. Most of these placements were to institutional settings. Only 4% involved the reconstitution of a family that had been separated.

Whether or not the family stayed together was clearly related to the identity of the sex offender (Table 7.9). Children who had been abused by step-parents or parents' lovers were least likely

Table 7.9. Change in Family Constellation Based on Victim's Relationship with the Offender

Offender Characteristics	Percent of Victims Living with Different Parents at Follow-Up
Natural parent	48%
Parent-figure	79%
Other relative	50%
Nonfamily	45%

to be living with the same parent-figures at follow-up. This finding is not surprising, given the earlier observation that substitute fathers were most likely to flee from the family when the allegations of sexual abuse came to light. However, the relatively high rate of family disruption (45%) when the offender was not part of the family is somewhat startling. It is impossible to determine how many of the families would have been changed by divorce or remarriage, regardless of the sexual abuse. However, these figures might also reinforce the notion that sexual abuse is indeed more prevalent in families with an unstable structure.

There was also evidence that the children who had experienced disruptions in their family environment exhibited more psychopathology at follow-up. Children who were living away from both parents had higher levels of emotional disturbance than those living in one- or two-parent families. Additionally, children who were no longer living in the same household were more disturbed than those who had remained with their families after the abuse. These data present the same interpretive difficulties as the findings about pathology and removal from the home at intake. One might speculate that some of the children were placed in institutional settings away from their parents because of the severity of their psychological difficulties. Nonetheless, there is little reason to believe that removing the child from the home in which she or he was abused necessarily reduced the danger of enduring psychological damage. It may be that the intervention occurred too late; some children had already suffered serious emotional harm before the sexual abuse came to light. In other instances, separation of the child from his or her family may actually have exacerbated their distress.

Use of Therapeutic Services
During Follow-Up

Although the FCP was based on a model of brief, focused intervention, the experiences with families suggested that most (78%) required further services once the initial intervention was concluded. Of course, referring a family for continued services and ensuring that they receive such services are entirely different matters. Thus, at follow-up an assessment was made of the extent to which families utilized social and mental health services after completing the FCP intervention.

As the data in Table 7.10 indicate, families received relatively few services during follow-up. Most (77%) had some contact with protective services. Indeed, contact with protective services was more common during follow-up than before the FCP treatment (i.e., 65%); although not all of the families had contact because of the sexual abuse. Some had an ongoing relationship with the agency owing to longstanding difficulties in providing adequate care for their children. Protective service involvement was more common among nonwhite families and those from the lower socioeconomic strata (Table 7.11). These findings are consistent with repeated observations that the poor and minorities who receive health care from public facilities are more likely to be subjected to official scrutiny than families who are able to seek private care.

The nature of the sexual abuse situation also influenced protective service involvement. In nearly all of the families in which the sexual offender was the child's natural or substitute father, there was some involvement with protective services. In contrast, in nearly half (47%) of the cases in which the offender was not a member of the family, there were no dealings with protective service personnel (see Table 7.12). It is also noteworthy that extensive

Table 7.10. Families' Use of Therapeutic Services During the Follow-Up Period

| | | Extent of Use | | |
| | | No Use at All | Limited Use | Extensive Use |
Services	Number of Cases	%	%	%
Protective Services	97	23	34	43
Private Social Services	90	86	6	8
Special Programs for Child:				
Drug abuse	91	99	1	0
Alcohol abuse	90	98	0	2
Delinquency	88	100	0	0
Runaway	88	98	2	0
Emergency shelter	88	90	10	0
Residential school	92	88	8	4
Psychotherapy				
at FCP	156	67	18	15
other facility	90	60	20	20

Table 7.11. Use of Protective Services and Characteristics of the Family

| | | Extent of Use | | |
Protective Services Utilized	Number of Cases	No Use at All %	Limited Use %	Extensive Use %
Social Class				
Business/Professional	12	17%	58%	25%
Skilled	20	60%	25%	15%
Semiskilled	22	14%	46%	41%
Unskilled	43	12%	26%	63%
Race				
White	75	25%	39%	36%
Nonwhite	22	14%	18%	68%

protective service involvement appeared to be more common when the offender was a parent surrogate rather than a natural parent. Although all cases of incest with a natural parent resulted in some contact with protective services, for the majority of the families

Table 7.12. Use of Protective Services and the Child's Relationship with
the Offender

		Extent of Use		
Relationship	Number of Cases	No Use at All	Limited Use	Extensive Use
Natural parent	19	0%	68%	37%
Parent-figure	22	14%	32%	55%
Other relative	20	20%	35%	45%
Nonfamily	32	47%	16%	38%

(68%) this contact was limited. In contrast, when the surrogate father was the abuser, the majority of families (55%) had extensive protective service contact. This is consistent with the findings already presented that children abused by surrogate parents were most disturbed when they entered treatment and that the mothers of these children were least supportive in dealing with the sexual abuse.

The only other resource used by a sizable portion of the sample was psychotherapy—15% of the cases were involved in FCP services on a regular basis for some part of the follow-up period; slightly more (20%) received some regular treatment at another mental health facility. There were no indications that the family's social characteristics influenced whether they received therapy. However, there was a tendency for families in which the child had been abused by a natural parent to obtain additional therapy, especially when cases continuing at the FCP were considered (see Table 7.13). The rates of regular therapy for families in which the natural father was an incest offender were nearly three times as high as those for families in which the child had been abused by an outsider.

The extent to which the victimized child and family members participated in psychotherapy was strongly related to the child's pathology. Children who had been most disturbed at the outset of FCP treatment were more likely to receive some type of therapy during the follow-up period. Similarly, those who appeared most disturbed at follow-up were also the children who had received more treatment. These findings can be readily interpreted. The

Table 7.13. Family Use of Therapy During Follow-Up, Based on Child's Relationship with the Offender

Relation of Offender to Child	Percent Using Therapy				Percent Using FCP Therapy			
	No. of Cases	No Therapy	Some Therapy	Regular Therapy	No.[1] of Cases	No Therapy	Some Therapy	Regular Therapy
Natural parent	17	12%	29%	59%	27	44%	30%	26%
Parent-figure	19	37%	21%	42%	30	77%	7%	17%
Other relative	22	27%	32%	41%	28	75%	7%	18%
Nonfamily	32	56%	22%	22%	45	64%	27%	9%

1. N's are larger because data were available on families who did not agree to follow-up.

children with greater emotional problems had a greater need for psychiatric intervention.

Perhaps the more important relationship between the child's pathology and treatment was that children who received more therapy at the FCP were also more likely to demonstrate improvements in psychopathology. Unfortunately, this relationship between treatment and improvement could not be generalized to children who had been involved in continued treatment outside of the FCP. This finding lends support to the idea that a specialized program such as the FCP can have a positive impact on the sexually abused child.

CONCLUSIONS

Data on the functioning of the sexually abused children in the 18-month period after revealing the sexual abuse and receiving crisis treatment suggests that 55% of the children did show a substantial diminution of emotional distress. Findings that greater improvements were associated with continued treatment at the FCP clinic support the belief that the program played a role in helping children recover from the emotional stresses of sexual victimization. Some of the distress aroused by the sexual victimization and reactions to its disclosure were reduced by treatment in a specialized clinic. It is noteworthy, however, that those who improved the most were likely to have continued in therapy beyond the initial crisis intervention. Perhaps in some of these cases the crisis treatment was instrumental in engaging families in longer-term treatment. By providing the family with support and assistance in dealing with the turmoil aroused by the sexual abuse, clinicians may also have increased the willingness of family members to examine their own more long-standing difficulties. This enhanced self-awareness may increase the likelihood for both parents and the victimized child to make use of therapeutic services to achieve significant changes in their lives.

It is important to realize, however, that there are also self-selection factors that influence whether or not a family continues in treatment and benefits from that treatment. Those families willing to invest time in resolving the difficulties associated with the sexual abuse are more likely to have the psychological strengths that maximize their capacity to benefit from treatment. Clinicians, too, may have placed greater emphasis on continuing treatment when they believed that the family had high prospects for effectively using the therapy. The improvements observed in the majority of the victims must be contrasted with the negative changes in a smaller number of cases (24%). Some of these instances of increased symptoms may reflect statistical artifacts or biases in measurement.

Nonetheless, it is likely that some of the victims genuinely did not benefit from treatment, and some even showed increasing psychopathology. Systematically distinguishing the characteristics or experiences of children who became worse from those who improved was beyond the scope of the current analyses. However, the available data and clinical observations allow some speculation about the factors that may increase the likelihood that a sexually victimized child will continue to exhibit problem behaviors. For some children, the sexual abuse may have been only one stressor in a terrible developmental history. As noted in Chapter 3, many of the children had histories of extensive physical abuse and severely disorganized home environments. During the follow-up, many children experienced continued environmental instability. One would not anticipate that a child with a long history of abuse and deprivation would obtain sufficient benefit, from brief crisis intervention or even from continued outpatient therapy, to counteract years of emotional trauma. Furthermore, it is unclear in such cases how much of the child's pathology was attributable to the sexual abuse. For a few of the children, sexual fondling may have been the *least* aggressive adult behavior to which they were subjected.

In other instances an increase in the child's difficulties during the follow-up period may have reflected reactions to the turmoil initiated by the disclosure of the sexual abuse. Some of the adolescents who were interviewed at follow-up (19%) indicated that they regretted having told about the sexual abuse. In some of these cases, the victims reported the abuse because they did not want to continue the sexual activity. They did not anticipate that the revelation might tear their families apart. In several cases in which the girl's father-figure faced prosecution, the victim became the focus of anger by other family members. Both mother and siblings held the victim responsible for the break-up of the family. Even in cases in which other family members were more supportive, the victim often felt torn between a wish to protect herself and guilt about harming her father.

Generalization of the results from this follow-up are limited by the relatively short time period and the absence of comparison with sexually abused children who did not receive treatment. It is impossible to judge whether some of the children who appeared asymptomatic one to two years after treatment may develop other difficulties later in life. Several studies of adult women who were victimized during childhood suggest that sexual dysfunction or other difficulties with heterosexual relationships often are sequelae of sexual abuse (Briere & Runtz, 1988; Fromuth, 1986; Herman, 1981; Meiselman, 1978, 1980). Relatively few of the victims in the present study were old enough to engage in consensual sexual relationships by the time they were re-evaluated. In addition, some of the more subtle effects of sexual abuse upon the victim's self-concept mentioned in the literature (e.g., the perception of herself as "dirty") may not be readily measured by scales tapping overt psychopathology.

Most of the published data on the long-term adverse effects of sexual abuse have been derived from samples of victims who received no treatment during childhood, but sought therapy as adults (Meiselman, 1978; Tsai et al., 1979). In contrast, all of the children in this study received some degree of therapeutic intervention, usually quite soon after the revelation of the sexual abuse. Again, one might speculate that the relatively low rates of significant psychiatric disturbance in these children were attributable to their having received therapy. One might also hypothesize that the seriously emotionally scarred adults high-lighted in other studies represent a relatively small subset of all victims, corresponding to those in this study who manifested the most difficulties and received the least help. In either case it is important to recognize that historical data on the effects of sexual abuse may be quite inconsistent with the results now being observed, because sexual abuse of children has become such a widely publicized, and hence much more frequently revealed, problem.

At this time, however, judgment must be reserved as there is no way to test our hypotheses. It is not possible to state with any certainty that children who do not receive services fare worse in the short- or long-run than those who are treated, and research designs that permit such comparison are either unfeasible or unethical. It is almost impossible to retrospectively evaluate treated and untreated victims because so few children had access to services until very recently. Prospectively studying treated and untreated victims by withholding interventions does not appear to be an ethically justifiable solution. Perhaps conducting longer-term follow-up studies of children who have participated in programs such as the FCP will yield greater insights into the eventual adjustment of sexually abused children.

EIGHT

Summary, Conclusions, and Recommendations

In the previous chapters, major findings associated with 156 sexually abused children treated at the Family Crisis Program were presented. The findings provide a profile of the kinds of children who are sexually abused, the nature and effects of the abuse, and the effects of crisis intervention. The present chapter provides a summary of these findings, their general implications for treatment, and recommendations for future research directions.

THE SEXUAL ABUSE VICTIM

The majority of children who were treated by the FCP were preadolescents, with 65% being younger than 13 years of age when they entered treatment. The age of these victims is consistent with the results from retrospective surveys of childhood sexual abuse experiences (Finkelhor, 1984; Russell, 1983; Wyatt, 1985) and calls into question earlier notions that offenders are enticed by an adolescent's budding sexuality. In agreement with earlier studies, girls were more likely to be victimized than boys. However, a comparison of the ratio of 3.5 girls to every boy in the FCP sample, with the ratios of approximately 2.5 females victims to each male in recent research suggests that some of the difference in rates of victimization may reflect a lowered probability of identifying and treating boys who have been victimized (Finkelhor, 1986; Risin & Koss, 1987; Vander Mey, 1988).

Data in the present study on the association of child sexual abuse, poverty, and family disruption are more controversial. There is no question that cases of child sexual abuse that reach treatment facilities represent a skewed sample of the sexual victimization that takes place. Findings from community surveys that child sexual abuse is unrelated to social class (Finkelhor, 1984; Peters, 1984; Russell, 1986) suggest that families with greater economic resources and stature in their communities may more easily escape the scrutiny of protective service investigations. However, the high levels of disruption in the family environments of the children seen by the Family Crisis Program—57% separated from a parent for more than six months before the age of six, 38% with a prior history of physical abuse or neglect—are much less readily interpreted as an artifact of sample selection. It appears more likely that a breakdown in stable family structure may increase a child's risk of being sexually victimized.

THE NATURE OF THE SEXUAL ABUSE

The majority of children (69%) treated at the FCP were subjected to repeated assaults over a period of months, and for 32% of the children, even years. In just 21% of the cases was the abuse limited to a single incident. The types of brief contacts with an exhibitionist that constitute as much as 44% of the childhood sexual victimization disclosed in community surveys (Badgley et al., 1984) represented only 4% of the cases referred to the FCP for treatment.

In the present study, the sexual abuse in 55% of the cases came to clinical attention because the child told someone, usually a parent or other relative. However, most children appear to be hesitant about revealing sexual abuse. Only 24% told immediately after the incident had occurred and 39% had not discussed the abuse with anyone before they came to the FCP clinic. An analysis of the circumstances distinguishing children who disclosed the abuse from those who did not suggests that both loyalty to the offender and fear of the offender's reaction to any disclosure play an important role in influencing victims to remain silent. These findings confirm the need for community educational programs that alert parents to signs that their children may have been victimized, as well as teach children how to bring their abuse to the attention of a responsive adult.

The Role of Force and Violence

Prior findings that children may passively comply with an adult's sexual overtures because of their own needs for attention or affection (e.g., DeFrancis, 1969) are challenged by the present findings. In 68% of the cases, the offender coerced the child to comply either through threats or actual physical aggression. Perhaps even more striking is the finding that parents were as likely as any other group of offenders to use violence. The importance of violence is further indicated by the fact that the degree of violence associated with the abuse was more important in determining the child's level of distress than the type of sexual act (e.g., fondling versus intercourse) or the duration of the abuse.

The Relationship Between Victim and Offender

The majority of victims treated at the FCP were sexually abused by a family member, including natural parents (19%), surrogate parents such as stepfathers or live-in boyfriends (21%), and other relatives (22%), while only 3% were victimized by strangers. Contrasting the relationships between offender and victim in the present sample with Finkelhor's (1984) community survey data showing 33% of adults revealing stranger victimization, and only 8% abuse by parental figures suggests that intrafamily sexual abuse or incest is disproportionately more likely to be referred for treatment. Even if the data from such community surveys are somewhat skewed by a respondent's reluctance to admit being sexually abused by his or her parents, the differences in the statistics suggest that many families may not seek professional intervention when a child has a single, isolated sexual experience with someone he or she does not know, unless the assault was particularly serious.

The impact of the child's relationship with the offender upon the degree of distress the child experiences was quite complex. Contrary to the inclinations of clinicians at the FCP to devote more services to families in which the sexual offender was the natural father, neither incest per se, nor closeness of the offender and child's relation was directly related to the child's manifest distress when she or he entered treatment. Children abused by a parent substitute (e.g., stepfather, parent's live-in partner) were the most severely disturbed. It is also noteworthy that children abused by parent substitutes had the least supportive mothers, and that lack of supportiveness was also associated with increased distress in the child. These findings together with evidence from survey data that children in families with stepfathers were at greater risk of being sexually abused either by the stepfather (Russell, 1986) or by others (Finkelhor, 1984; Gruber & Jones, 1983) highlight the significance of family intactness in some sexual abuse situations. Perhaps the lack of either a blood relationship or a long history of emotional attachment between a stepfather and his children diminishes the willingness or capacity to serve as a protector of the children. At the same time, mothers who have formed new relationships may feel greater conflict between allegiances to the children from their previous marriages and their new partners.

LEVELS OF DISTRESS AMONG THE VICTIMS

FCP's assessment of the sexual abuse victims with standardized measures of psychopathology at the time they entered treatment indicated that the level of psychological distress varied from complete absence of any conventional childhood symptoms to extreme and pervasive emotional problems, with 27% of the overall sample exhibiting clinically significant levels of symptoms. Because the research design did not permit FCP to isolate pathology resulting from the abuse from preexisting problems, the percentage of children with obvious psychopathology is probably an overestimate of the number who developed the symptoms as a consequence of the sexual abuse.

Comparing the extent to which children exhibit clinical psychopathology with their parents' estimates—that 33% of the victims were severely harmed and 67% would experience difficulties in later life because of the abuse—raises interesting questions about how the impact of sexual abuse is best assessed. It is likely that aspects of emotional health that might be influenced by sexual abuse, such as a child's ability to trust adults or to develop emotionally gratifying relationships that are not exploitative, cannot be measured by symptom checklists. However, it is equally plausible that the emotional distress of some parents upon learning that their child has been victimized may excessively heighten their vigilance for signs of distress in the child, as well as their fears that the child will suffer future difficulties because of the abuse.

Assuming there is a genuine continuum of responses to sexual abuse, the FCP research findings suggest that several factors may explain why some children exhibit serious emotional problems while others do not. As noted above, both the aggressiveness of the sexual assault and the degree to which the victim's mother responded to the abuse in an unsupportive way were associated with greater distress in the child. Several other factors that appeared to mediate the child's response to the sexual abuse are discussed below.

Age at Commencement of Treatment

First of all, the age of the child at the time when clinical services are initially offered may be an important factor. Relatively few preschool youngsters (17%) demonstrated sufficient behavioral problems to be designated as seriously disturbed. However, clinical observations and the follow-up data suggest that some of the youngest victims may exhibit more serious problems later in their development. In contrast to the low levels of serious emotional disturbance found in preschool children, severe psychological difficulties appear to be quite frequent (40%) in youngsters in the 7- to 13-year-old group. Differences between preschool and school-aged youngsters suggest that adolescents, who are at an even higher level of cognitive development and are more likely to have been abused for longer periods of time, ought to respond most intensely to sexual abuse. It was somewhat surprising, therefore, that so few of the adolescent victims in this study (8%) exhibited severe pathology. There are two possible explanations for this finding. First, children who are victimized in adolescence may be better able to cognitively process the experience. And second, it is possible that some of the most severely disturbed victims were not treated at the FCP because their acting out behavior made them inappropriate candidates for noncoercive, outpatient treatment.

Children Removed from Home

Evaluations at both intake and follow-up showed that children who were removed from their homes because of sexual abuse manifested greater distress than those who remained. These findings are difficult to interpret, as the decision to place a child outside the home might have been based on the fact that she or he was already manifesting signs of severe emotional problems. However, the evidence of greater distress in children removed from their homes, in conjunction with data showing that the percent of children living away from their parents had increased from 9% at intake into the FCP program to 24% at follow-up raises questions about the family disruption that so often accompanies the disclosure of sexual abuse. If removing the child from the home can exacerbate the level of stress for the child, it is important for both clinicians and policymakers to examine whether there are appropriate alternatives to removal, and if not, to determine when removal of the child is absolutely essential to ensure personal safety.

Disclosure of the Abuse

Findings of less anxiety and anger among children who never told of the sexual abuse suggest that disclosure of the abuse may not necessarily provide immediate relief. At times, it may even temporarily increase the level of stress for the child. The finding, for example, that mothers of children abused by a parent substitute showed greater anger and less protectiveness for the child when the abuse was disclosed than other mothers is somewhat consistent with clinical theories that point to the collusive role that mothers sometime play in maintaining the abuse (Kempe, 1978; Peters, 1976). The majority of mothers (81%), however, demonstrated at least a moderate degree of concern for the child when the victimization was disclosed. Relatively few (30%) punished the child when told about the abuse, and even fewer (18%) failed to take any action to protect the child. Furthermore, mothers of incest victims were no more likely to be unsupportive than were mothers of children who had been abused by acquaintances and strangers. Similarly, although 41% of the mothers had been childhood sexual abuse victims themselves, victimized mothers did not respond differently than those who had no history of sexual abuse.

The potential, however, for increased stress when the child discloses the sexual abuse is further emphasized by the findings that most parents who came to FCP felt that the sexual abuse clearly had a harmful impact upon the child; 60% of the parents believed that the sexual abuse and its disclosure were the worst events that had occurred in the family during the past three years (i.e., the period approximately 18 months pre-FCP and 18 months after beginning FCP). Simultaneously, 67% felt that the abuse would cause difficulties for the child's future life. Thus, 78% of the parents believed that the sexual abuse itself had a harmful impact on the child and even more (88%) believed the family had been harmed by the abuse. A substantial proportion of the parents felt that the disclosure of the abuse caused some degree of harm for the family (43%) or the victimized child (36%).

The extent to which parents believed that the children were harmed by the experience and would continue to experience harmful effects later in life is quite striking. Indeed, considerably more parents were likely to see their children as damaged-for-life than the measures of clinical psychopathology would suggest. Perhaps some parents were attuned to changes in the child's attitudes and self-perceptions that were not expressed through overt behavioral disturbances. In this respect, researchers, by relying upon signs of classic psychopathology, may be underestimating the degree of emotional distress that a victim experiences. The child who appears to be an obedient, hard-working student seldom elicits the attention of psychiatric professionals. However, this same child may be experiencing severe emotional pain because of the abuse.

A second explanation for the dire predictions regarding the effects of sexual victimization is that some parents were reacting more to their own preconceptions about sexual exploitation than to the child's actual behavior. In a number of cases, when the family entered FCP treatment, the major focus of attention was the parents' distress about the abuse. For example, one mother became extremely upset when she discovered that her 13-year-old daughter was sexually involved with the 21-year-old husband of an aunt. In contrast, the girl perceived her "abuser" as a "boyfriend." In cases such as this, a parent's reactions may be influenced more by a belief that something "bad" or "wrong" has occurred, than by signs that the child is in distress. A parent may thereby conclude that the child must have been harmed because sexual exploitation is such an outrage to the parent's values.

In some cases, a parent's anxiety that a child has been or will be damaged by sexual abuse may also prompt the parent to respond in ways that may actually increase the child's distress. For example, several mothers of preschool victims were so fearful that their children might be reabused, they persisted in questioning their children about possible sexual overtures by adults.

If some parents do overestimate the extent to which the sexual abuse has affected their child, there is the possibility that their expectations will set into motion a self-fulfilling prophecy. Parents who expect their child to be scarred may treat him or her differently. The extreme of this attitude was most starkly illustrated by a mother's contention that she could no longer care about her victimized 8-year-old daughter because the child had been "ruined."

Although very few parents believed their child's sexual abuse had any redeeming aspects, a substantial number indicated that bringing the abuse into the open helped both the child and the family. At follow-up, for example, while 45% of the families still felt that the child was harmed by disclosure of the abuse, 44% stated that the child was actually helped by disclosure. There are many reasons why a parent might perceive disclosure of sexual abuse as helpful. Many parents felt the disclosure of the abuse permitted them to come to the assistance of their child. In a number of families where incestuous sexual abuse had occurred, both the mother who was unaware of the abuse, and the father who felt conflicted about his behavior, experienced some relief after the sexual activity had come to light and they were offered professional assistance. Of course, the relief associated with exploring new options for relating to each other as a family may have come after considerable turmoil, as the earlier discussion of the mother's responses illustrated. However, during the follow-up period some of the families may have begun to experience some satisfactions in their new, nonexploitative patterns of relating to one another.

Even in cases where the sexual offender was not a member of the child's nuclear family, the disclosure of the abuse sometimes brought into focus family problems that could be addressed in treatment. For example, family sessions were held with the parents and siblings of a 16-year-old girl who was raped after she surreptitiously traveled with a friend from her suburban home to a dangerous downtown area. In attempting to understand the effects of the rape and what had motivated the girl to place herself in a dangerous situation, family members were able to explore some of the ongoing conflicts and difficulties in communication that existed between the parents and the children.

Although a substantial proportion of families felt the disclosure of the sexual abuse was helpful, a similar number experienced it as a harmful event. Experiences in some of these cases were more similar to the accounts of poor institutional management of sexual abuse: children precipitously removed from the home before a thorough investigation, or pressure on the child from a variety of investigative agencies to describe the incident repeatedly. In other instances, families associated the revelation of the abuse with dramatic psychiatric decompensation in family members, especially the offender. Several fathers became suicidal or required psychiatric hospitalization after their incestuous activities were exposed.

Whether disclosure of sexual abuse serves to mobilize a family's strengths as they work to resolve the problem or to intensify stresses upon the child and the family unit may depend upon both the quality of the resources that are available and the psychological capacities of the family members. Because all families in this study received specialized treatment to help them deal with the crises raised by disclosure of the abuse, it is impossible to assess whether the same proportion would have felt the disclosure was helpful if no treatment had been forthcoming. It is also important to recognize that while the initial impact of disclosure may be extremely disruptive for all family members, a child who continues to keep the abuse secret while allowing the activity to continue may suffer long-term traumatic consequences. The same potential for long-term harm may even be true for the child who does not have the opportunity to work through the feelings associated with the sexual abuse that occurred in the past. If there is some resolution of the stress associated with the abuse once disclosed, it is possible that the family may realize wider opportunities for improving intrafamilial relationships.

IMPLICATIONS FOR TREATMENT

Although the FCP research was not designed to compare treated victims with a control group, an evaluation of the treatment sample at the conclusion of the crisis intervention, and at the 18-month follow-up, allows some conclusions about the impact of intervention on sexually abused children. At the conclusion of crisis treatment, clinicians indicated that 76% of the families had benefited at least moderately from treatment. At follow-up, even more families (82%) indicated that their contact with the FCP either in crisis treatment or continued therapy had been at least somewhat helpful. A further assessment of the victim's behavior with standardized measures was, however, somewhat less positive. In all, 55% of the children achieved reductions in symptoms and 57% improvements in self-concept that were greater than could be expected by chance.

In examining the results of this study, it is important to recognize that conclusions about the association between FCP interventions and improvements in the sexually abused children must be tentative. Because FCP was unable to compare the children who were treated at the FCP with sexual abuse victims who received either no treatment or alternative interventions, it is difficult to determine if the changes in the children's well-being necessarily resulted from the FCP treatment. This proviso is especially important because many of the families received a variety of other services during and after their FCP treatment. In addition, some of the changes in children's behavior, both positive and negative, may be the result of natural maturational processes.

Although these data do not allow one to state with conviction that the FCP treatment did cause the changes observed during the 18-month period following treatment, they highlight very important issues in the treatment of sexual abuse. One can begin to understand the kinds of changes in a child's life that may occur following intervention for sexual abuse, what types of interventions a family will experience as useful, and what circumstances may enhance or impede reduction of a child's distress.

Perhaps even more important than the rates of improvement in the treated cases were observations derived from the research about the varied treatment needs of sexually abused children and their families. These observations, based upon both the research data and clinical judgments about the treatment process, result in the conclusions described below.

CONCLUSIONS

A classic crisis intervention model is applicable only to a limited range of cases. The family crisis treatment model, based upon classic crisis intervention theory (Caplan, 1964), viewed the occurrence or disclosure of sexual abuse as a crisis that disrupts a family's ongoing coping mechanisms. Experiences with the families in the study revealed major differences between the premises of traditional crisis theory and the clinical reality of sexually abused children. Sexual abuse is rarely an isolated catastrophe that disrupts an otherwise normal family adaptation. Only in cases in which the abuse consisted of a single isolated incident in a family that was basically psychologically healthy did a 12-session crisis intervention suffice to restore the family to adequate functioning.

Analyses of the relationship between treatment success and the characteristics of the family indicate that the capacity to obtain some benefit from treatment is not diminished by a family's history of prior problems or the severity of the sexual abuse situation. However, the extent to which families can achieve adequate functioning following the crisis intervention is clearly influenced by these factors. Children who were not physically harmed during the course of the abuse, those who were victimized by acquaintances and strangers rather than family members, and those who came from families with no prior history of psychiatric or social services were most likely to function adequately.

In the majority of cases, however, crisis intervention was not enough; 78% of the families required referral for further services. For some of these families, the revelation of sexual abuse was only the most recent in a long series of psychological and social disruptions in their lives. In these cases, a breakdown in coping mechanisms was a chronic condition that could not be reversed with crisis intervention alone. Data from the clinicians revealed that very few families (9%) were able to achieve the ideal goal of crisis intervention, that is, a return to adequate functioning in their daily lives without therapeutic support.

Although crisis treatment alone may not be sufficient in most cases of sexual abuse, the initial crisis work may be instrumental in engaging families in a longer-term treatment process. By providing the family with support and assistance in dealing with the immediate issues raised by the disclosure of the abuse, clinicians may also increase the willingness of families to work on longstanding difficulties. However, it is important to recognize that there are also self-selection factors that influence whether or not a family remains and benefits from treatment. Those families who are most willing to invest time in resolving the difficulties associated with the sexual abuse may be more likely to have the psychological strengths that maximize their capacity to benefit from therapy.

It is also important to distinguish cases in which sexual abuse is the focal family problem (usually instances of parent-child incest) from those in which an incident of sexual victimization is only one limited aspect of a chaotic family history. It is noteworthy that fully 40% of the families followed did not believe that the sexual abuse or its revelation were the worst things that had happened to the family. The goal of sexual abuse treatment programs with multiproblem families may be to deal only with the immediate crises caused by the abuse before referring the family to a set of psychiatric and social service agencies that are prepared to offer long-term support.

Collaboration between treatment and child protective services is essential. In their role as official investigators of child sexual abuse, protective services were perceived by families as harmful more often than any other agency involved in sexual abuse (29%). Furthermore, the children removed from their homes by protective services seemed to exhibit more severe emotional distress. This does not mean that protective service agencies should abdicate their role of interceding in families to ensure the safety of a child, but rather that sexual abuse treatment programs should work closely with protective services to determine when therapeutic work with a family can be a better alternative to disrupting family ties.

A strong treatment focus on parents of the sexually abused child is necessary if a family is to stay together. Evaluation of the mother must include an assessment of her capacity to work through her own distress about the sexual abuse if she is to be able both to protect her child physically and to support her child emotionally. If the father or father substitute is also the offender, his capacity to control his behavior must be determined. In the absence of an active treatment involvement on the part of a father-figure who has sexually offended, treatment staff may work with the mother, protective services, and legal agencies to remove the father, rather than the child, from the home. Thus, only in those cases in which treatment staff have determined that neither parent is capable of protecting the child from continued sexual abuse will protective services need to resort to removing the child.

Treatment programs must recognize parents' need for support. The sexual abuse of a child creates many intense feelings in the child's parents: anxiety about the extent to which the child may be "harmed for life," guilt about not preventing the abuse, anger toward the offender, and sometimes even anger toward the child. The responses by parents to the abuse may have a powerful impact upon the child. As the data show, a punitive, angry mother may heighten a child's level of distress. Parental anxieties may also prompt persistent probing to determine whether the child is at risk for further abuse. Particularly in cases of preschool children who have suffered a brief victimization and show few initial symptoms, this type of response may interfere with any healthy efforts to put the experience in the past and forget about it.

Helping parents to understand and deal with their own feelings about the abuse is essential if they are to become allies in comforting and protecting the child. Some parents may need an opportunity to discuss their feelings, while others may require more concrete education about ways in which to help the child. Sensitive work with parents is particularly important when the abuse has raised a conflict between allegiances to the child and the offender.

Finally, increased efforts at prevention of child sexual abuse may be the best long-term way to avoid the stresses that many child victims suffer. Public education programs are necessary to alert parents and other caregivers, such as teachers, medical personnel, and clergy, to signs that a child may have been victimized or may be in danger of being sexually abused. In addition, parents need to be alerted to the importance of taking a child's allegations of sexual abuse seriously and responding supportively. Educational efforts with children should be devoted to helping them to identify inappropriate sexual overtures and to feel free to report approaches. Groups throughout the country have been developing movies and theatrical performances that sensitively deal with the topic of sexual abuse for child audiences (see review by Finkelhor, 1986). Because it is important that wide groups of children are exposed to such educational material, communities should consider including sexual abuse prevention programs in school curriculums.

RECOMMENDATIONS FOR FUTURE RESEARCH DIRECTIONS

As noted in earlier chapters, the design of the current research placed limitations upon the types of inferences that could be drawn from the data. First of all, the absence of a control group made it impossible to determine the extent to which the changes observed in the sample were attributable to the FCP intervention. One could argue that in the absence of any therapy, some proportion of sexually abused children would improve simply with the passage of time. However, developing a study with an untreated control group raises significant ethical issues.

Second, large amounts of missing data, especially for fathers of abuse victims, precluded conducting important analyses. For example, when all subjects with unknown information on any variable were deleted from the sample, the remaining group was too small to permit multivariate analyses. Thus, the FCP was unable to explore potentially complex relationships among the factors that influence a child's reaction to abuse. In addition, a number of constraints in the FCP data collection procedure interfered with obtaining complete data for all cases. However, much of the missing information is an inevitable consequence of the nature of sexual abuse. When researchers attempt to collect a broad representation of the types of sexual abuse that come to clinical attention, there will inevitably be cases in which information is incomplete. Some details of the abuse cannot be collected because the child is too young to explain completely. Other details are not remembered because the abuse started so far in the past, while others will not be revealed because the victim fears the reaction of the offender. Similarly, data about the fathers of abuse victims (crucial to testing much of the clinical theorizing about incest) may be unavailable because the fathers have broken off all contact with the family long before the treatment or research commences.

In evaluating the shortcomings of the current study and proposing alternative approaches for further research, it is important to recognize that systematic research on treatment of child sexual abuse is quite a new endeavor. Investigators have few standards to call upon in designing a study. Indeed, there is still considerable debate about the activities that should be included in the definition of sexual abuse (Finkelhor, 1986). However, our experiences with the FCP have suggested several profitable avenues for future research.

1. *Comparative Treatment Outcome Studies.* As more approaches to treating sexual abuse are being developed, it may soon be possible to develop studies in which victims and their families are randomly assigned to alternative treatment strategies. This approach would avoid the ethical issues of deliberately withholding treatment, while at the same time providing an opportunity to more rigorously test the efficacy of treatments.

2. *Longitudinal Studies.* As identification of sexually abused children and programs for treating them have increased, there are more sources of subjects for prospective rather than retrospective studies of the longer-term effects of sexual abuse. Much of the previous research on the long-term effects of childhood sexual abuse has relied upon adult recall of the childhood emotional trauma or has measured emotional dysfunction in women who have already identified themselves as candidates for psychiatric services. Conducting follow-up studies comparing children who have received treatment with those who have not, as they manage the passage into adolescence and adulthood, would provide data on the long-term effects of sexual abuse that is not biased by either faulty recall of distant experiences or selection of subjects who are disproportionately more likely to show serious emotional problems.

3. *Large Collaborative Studies.* Results from the present study suggest that the impact of a sexual abuse experience is influenced

by complex interactions of factors. For example, duration of the abuse may interact with the age at which it started so that some combinations of these two factors have different effects than others. However, statistically testing for these interactions requires larger samples of research subjects than are usually available from one clinical setting. Collaborative studies, in which carefully defined samples of victims from several different clinical settings are assessed with the same measures, would provide a means for developing a large enough data base to explore interactions among potential sources of trauma.

4 *Standardization of Measures.* Building a cumulative body of knowledge about child sexual abuse will also be facilitated when individual investigators begin to use a set of common measures. At present, emotional trauma in sexually abused children is measured either with standardized scales of childhood psychopathology (such as the Louisville Behavior Checklist used in this study) or nonstandardized measures of symptoms associated with sexual abuse developed by individual researchers. The disadvantage of the standardized scales is that they may not precisely tap the particular constellations of problems that clinicians have identified in cases of sexual abuse. On the other hand, specialized measures do not readily permit comparisons between studies if each investigator has a different set of questions.

5. *Specially Focused Studies.* It is unclear how many more global studies of the entire range of child sexual abuse are necessary to establish a body of knowledge about the overall phenomenon of sexual exploitation of children. The time is approaching when some investigators should begin to develop in-depth explorations of a much narrower segment of the sexual abuse problem. For example, the consistent association between heightened risk for abuse and the presence of a stepfather in the family in previous studies (Finkelhor, 1986; Phelan, 1986) suggests the need for a more detailed study of the similarities and differences between father-child and stepfather-child incest. A further avenue for exploration is suggested by the data in this study of two typical patterns of symptoms in school-age victims—anxious, inhibited versus aggressive, acting out. Data on the differences in either the nature

of the sexual abuse or the child's history that predispose a victim to respond with one constellation of symptoms rather than the other is essential if the initial and long-term effects of child sexual abuse are to be adequately dealt with in the years ahead.

Data Analyses for Chapter 4

Analyses of the relationships among cetain aspects of sex abuse and reactions to the abuse entailed analyses of variance in which a measure of the abuse that could be represented as a continuous variable (e.g., duration of the abuse, mothers' reactions) served as a dependent variable; and a categorical variable, such as the child's relationship with the offender, served to identify contrast groups. The following tables include data for the major contrasts that were reported in the text of Chapter 4.

Table A.1. Correlations Among Sex Abuse Variables

	Injury	Recency	Duration	Age Began
Degree of Physical Injury (N = 138)				
Recency of Abuse (N = 144)	−.07			
Duration of Abuse (N = 141)	−.07	.29***		
Age When Abuse Began (N = 131)	−.00	.12	.14	
Frequency of Abuse (N = 140)	.03	.38***	.55***	−.01

	Correlation of Age at Intake with Sex Abuse				
	Injury	Recency	Duration	Age Began	Frequency
Age at Intake	.00	.24**	.34***	.88***	.23

* $p < .05$; ** $p < .01$; *** $p < .001$

Table A.2. Analyses of Variance: Influence of Child's Sex
on Sex Abuse Variables

		Female	Male	df	F
Degree of	(N)	107	31		
Physical	M	1.39	1.13	1,137	4.28*
Injury	SD	.68	.34		
Recency of	(N)	112	32		
the Abuse	M	2.65	2.53	1,143	<1
	SD	1.09	.95		
Duration of	(N)	111	30		
the Abuse	M	2.59	2.37	1,140	<1
	SD	1.56	1.16		
Age When	(N)	101	30		
the Abuse	M	9.20	8.60	1,130	<1
Began	SD	3.71	4.08		
Frequency of	(N)	110	30		
the Abuse	M	1.89	1.63	1,139	<1
	SD	1.72	1.47		

* $p < .05$; ** $p < .01$; *** $p < .001$

Table A.3. Analyses of Variance: Influence of Child's Race
on Sex Abuse Variables

		White	Nonwhite	df	F
Degree of	(N)	107	31		
Physical	M	1.26	1.58	1,137	6.37*
Injury	SD	.59	.72		
Recency of	(N)	106	38		
the Abuse	M	2.65	2.53	1,143	<1
	SD	1.01	1.18		
Duration of	(N)	107	34		
the Abuse	M	2.55	2.53	1,140	<1
	SD	1.49	1.46		
Age When	(N)	97	34		
the Abuse	M	9.43	8.00	1,130	3.67
Began	SD	3.66	4.00		
Frequency of	(N)	106	34		
the Abuse	M	1.92	1.56	1,139	1.24
	SD	1.64	1.73		

* $p < .05$; ** $p < .01$; *** $p < .001$

Table A.4. Analyses of Variance: Influence of Type of Sexual Act
on Sex Abuse Variables

		Intercourse	Penetration	Fondling, Masturb.	Noncontact	df	F
Degree of	(N)	34	56	33	9		
Physical	M	1.88	1.25	1.03	1.11	3,131	15.06***
Injury	SD	.81	.55	.17	.33		
Recency of	(N)	42	55	35	8		
the Abuse	M	2.69	2.56	2.80	2.25	3,139	<1
	SD	1.09	.98	1.18	.89		
Duration of	(N)	41	54	33	8		
the Abuse	M	2.63	2.70	2.58	1.32	3,132	<1
	SD	1.62	1.41	2.00	1.60		
Age When	(N)	38	51	30	8		
Abuse	M	10.11	8.16	9.13	10.50	3,126	2.36
Began	SD	3.52	3.88	4.01	2.67		
Frequency of	(N)	41	54	33	8		
the Abuse	M	1.93	2.11	1.76	.75	3,135	1.68
	SD	1.75	1.51	1.75	1.49		

* $p < .05$; ** $p < .01$; *** $p < .001$

Table A.5. Influence of Offender's Relationship to Child
on Sex Abuse Variables

		Natural Parent	Parent Figure Not Blood Relative	Other Relative	Nonfamily	df	F
Degree of	(N)	28	27	33	45		
Physical	M	1.18	1.48	1.33	1.38	3,132	1.09
Injury	SD	.48	.75	.60	.68		
Recency of	(N)	27	31	31	51		
the Abuse	M	2.89	2.42	2.90	2.43	3,139	2.25
	SD	.93	.85	1.22	1.12		
Duration of	(N)	24	31	32	50		
the Abuse	M	2.92	3.09	2.75	1.96	3,136	5.22**
	SD	1.67	1.49	1.48	1.16		
Age When	(N)	24	30	26	47		
Abuse	M	8.21	10.43	8.77	8.70	3,126	1.96
Began	SD	4.04	3.61	3.57	3.74		
Frequency of	(N)	24	31	32	50		
the Abuse	M	2.33	1.87	2.38	1.34	3,136	3.49*
	SD	1.63	1.59	1.52	1.69		

* $p < .05$; ** $p < .01$; *** $p < .001$

Table A.6. The Effect of the Length of Time Until the Child Revealed the Sexual Abuse on Sex Abuse Variables

		Immediately	Later	Never	df	F
Degree of	(N)	36	52	50		
Physical	M	1.50	1.15	1.40	2,137	3.78*
Injury	SD	.81	.41	.63		
Recency of	(N)	37	55	52		
Abuse	M	2.08	2.98	2.63	2,143	8.93***1
	SD	.83	1.10	1.01		
Duration of	(N)	36	57	48		
Abuse	M	1.61	3.21	2.46	2,140	15.74***1
	SD	1.08	1.37	1.49		
Age When	(N)	37	46	48		
Abuse	M	9.19	9.35	8.68	2,130	<1
Began	SD	4.07	3.74	3.67		
Frequency of	(N)	36	57	47		
Abuse	M	.61	2.72	1.70	2,139	23.80***1
	SD	.87	1.52	1.68		

* $p < .05$; ** $p < .01$; *** $p < .001$
1. Artifact of definition of immediate revelation.

Table A.7. Influence of a Change in the Family Because of Sexual Abuse on Sex Abuse Variables

		No	Yes, Child Removed	Yes, Parent Changed	df	F
Degree of	(N)	82	22	34		
Physical	M	1.21	1.45	1.56	2,137	4.41*
Injury	SD	.51	.74	.75		
Recency of	(N)	74	32	37		
Abuse	M	2.43	2.78	2.89	2,142	2.81
	SD	.94	1.29	1.02		
Duration of	(N)	75	32	33		
Abuse	M	2.09	3.03	3.06	2,139	7.93***
	SD	1.29	1.73	1.34		
Age When	(N)	71	26	33		
Abuse	M	8.68	9.15	9.64	2,129	<1
Began	SD	4.03	3.22	3.59		
Frequency of	(N)	74	32	33		
Abuse	M	1.45	2.06	2.54	2,138	5.69**
	SD	1.48	1.81	1.68		

* $p < .05$; ** $p < .01$; *** $p < .001$

APPENDIX B

Data Analyses for Chapter 5

The primary objective of these statistical analyses was to measure the extent to which aspects of the sexual abuse a child experienced accounted for variability in psychopathology at the time the child entered the Family Crisis Program. Because analyses indicated that the age of the child upon initial evaluation had an impact on the types of symptoms and the degree of distress the child expressed, the analyses required some control for the age of the victim. Thus, two statistical strategies were selected. With measures of the sexual abuse that were rated on ordinal scales, such as mothers' responses to the abuse, partial correlations were performed. These analyses assessed the relationship between each dimension of the sex abuse and each measure of the child's psychological state, controlling for the child's age at the time of intake. With measures of the sexual abuse that were categorical, such as relationship with the offender, analyses of covariance were performed. In these analyses, the categories of the sexual abuse measure served as levels of the independent variable: age was the covariate, and the level of the child's pathology was the dependent variable. In the tables reporting analysis of variance, means are based on uncorrected scores. However, there were no instances in which removing the effects of age eliminated the effect that had proved to be significant with a univariate analysis of variance.

Table B.1. Partial Correlations Between Aspects of the Sexual Abuse and Pathology in the Child, Controlling for the Child's Age at the Time of Intake

Pathology Scales	Features of Abuse			
	Child's Age at Start (N = 131)	Duration (N = 141)	Extent of Physical Injury (N = 138)	Aggression Involved (N = 156)
Louisville Total Severity Level (N = 112)	.06	-.01	.29**	.02
Louisville Factors: E-1 and E-2 (N = 88)				
Aggression	.18	-.10	.22*	.15
Emotional Distress	.10	-.06	.20*	.01
Severe Symptoms	.18	-.06	.28**	-.07
School Problems	.18	-.10	.32**	.16
Gottschalk: (N = 88)				
Anxiety	-.15	.06	.02	.11
Hostility Directed Out	-.15	.09	.13	.15
Hostility Directed In	.09	.03	.00	.12
Ambivalent Hostility	-.17	.04	.09	.20*
Total Hostility	-.13	.07	.11	.21*
Self-Concept (N = 123)	-.06	.11	-.04	-.03

* $p < .05$; ** $p < .01$; *** $p < .001$

Table B.2. Analyses of Covariance:
Influence of Worst Sex Act on Pathology

Pathology Scales		Intercourse	Penetration	Fondling	No Contact	F (df)
			Sex Act			
Louisville Total Severity Level		(N = 26)	(N = 44)	(N = 27)	(N = 9)	(3,105)
(N = 112)	M	45.91	44.01	43.05	43.98	<1
	SD	(9.05)	(11.69)	(8.95)	(11.95)	
Louisville Factors: E-1 and E-2						
(N = 88)		(N = 20)	(N = 36)	(N = 20)	(N = 7)	(3,82)
Aggression	M	63.76	60.56	57.06	59.18	<1
	SD	(17.08)	(17.58)	(13.66)	(12.68)	
Emotional Distress	M	55.94	56.02	54.58	50.81	<1
	SD	(11.76)	(11.27)	(11.50)	(7.52)	
Severe Symptoms	M	65.79	66.51	62.63	59.86	<1
	SD	(13.32)	(18.60)	(17.71)	(13.14)	
School Problems	M	60.73	59.38	57.63	57.19	<1
	SD	(12.84)	(14.80)	(11.44)	(10.10)	
Gottschalk: (N = 88)		(N = 24)	(N = 32)	(N = 19)	(N = 7)	(3,81)
Anxiety	M	46.78	48.66	54.21	40.06	3.68*
	SD	(12.49)	(8.71)	(9.44)	(10.93)	
Hostility Directed In	M	53.83	54.27	54.38	52.39	<1
	SD	(15.17)	(14.36)	(15.60)	(12.96)	
Hostility Directed Out	M	60.67	58.33	56.15	55.13	<1
	SD	(21.65)	(14.40)	(15.19)	(7.89)	
Ambivalent Hostility	M	58.86	55.20	61.93	51.91	<1
	SD	(25.00)	(20.95)	(23.65)	(15.19)	
Total Hostility	M	57.79	55.93	57.49	53.14	<1
	SD	(17.03)	(10.99)	(13.37)	(9.50)	
Self-Concept		(N = 34)	(N = 48)	(N = 28)	(N = 8)	(3,117)
(N = 123)	M	52.97	52.35	49.91	50.11	<1
	SD	(7.79)	(7.93)	(12.66)	(12.73)	

* $p < .05$

Table B.3. Analyses of Covariance:
Influence of Relationship with Offender on Pathology

Pathology Scales		Natural Parent	Parent Surrogate	Other Relative	Nonrelative	F
Louisville Total Severity Level		(N = 20)	(N = 24)	(N = 27)	(N = 36)	
	M	41.00	45.62	45.92	43.65	1.67
	SD	(10.58)	(12.41)	(10.78)	(8.17)	
Louisville Factors: E-1 and E-2						
(N = 88)		(N = 17)	(N = 11)	(N = 21)	(N = 34)	(3,82)
Aggression	M	53.81	76.34	60.64	59.67	4.29**
	SD	(13.74)	(24.75)	(13.93)	(14.60)	
Emotional Distress	M	52.64	61.88	54.95	54.13	1.64
	SD	(12.33)	(14.45)	(9.76)	(9.91)	
Severe Symptoms	M	59.28	74.56	62.49	65.38	1.97
	SD	(17.35)	(26.27)	(9.79)	(14.94)	
School Problems	M	53.67	70.42	60.78	56.59	4.77**
	SD	(11.64)	(20.48)	(9.89)	(10.24)	
Gottschalk: (N = 88)		(N = 19)	(N = 21)	(N = 17)	(N = 27)	(3,83)
Anxiety	M	46.15	49.67	50.38	46.17	<1
	SD	(14.52)	(8.83)	(7.68)	(10.99)	
Hostility Directed Out	M	58.76	56.44	57.57	57.71	<1
	SD	(15.08)	(13.16)	(23.09)	(15.91)	
Hostility Directed In	M	54.61	52.44	55.10	50.37	<1
	SD	(11.59)	(15.45)	(15.14)	(14.63)	
Ambivalent Hostility	M	60.61	56.75	53.13	55.51	<1
	SD	(30.11)	(20.40)	(19.25)	(19.55)	
Total Hostility	M	57.99	55.21	55.27	54.53	<1
	SD	(15.78)	(10.12)	(13.34)	(13.76)	
Self-Concept		(N = 26)	(N = 28)	(N = 27)	(N = 38)	(3,118)
(N = 123)	M	54.15	47.66	52.32	53.78	2.97*
	SD	(8.26)	(9.49)	(11.58)	(7.89)	

* $p < .05$; ** $p < .01$; *** $p < .001$

Table B.4. Analyses of Covariance:
Influence of Child's Revelation of Abuse on Pathology

Pathology Scales		Immediately	Later	Never	F F (df)
			When Child Revealed:		
Louisville Total Severity Level		(N = 31)	(N = 45)	(N = 36)	(2,111)
(N = 112)	M	43.57	43.53	45.12	
	SD	(10.16)	(10.04)	(10.86)	<1
Louisville E-1 and E-2		(N = 27)	(N = 29)	(N = 32)	(2,87)
Aggression	M	60.46	63.05	58.82	<1
	SD	(18.89)	(17.25)	(13.88)	
Emotional Distress	M	54.72	54.16	56.44	<1
	SD	(12.72)	(10.55)	(10.36)	
Serious Pathology	M	63.65	63.37	65.63	<1
	SD	(18.17)	(14.86)	(17.27)	
School Problems	M	59.69	58.18	58.78	<1
	SD	(15.69)	(11.66)	(12.29)	
Gottschalk		(N = 19)	(N = 39)	(N = 30)	(2,87)
Anxiety	M	50.76	50.11	43.26	4.06*
	SD	(10.53)	(9.75)	(12.05)	
Hostility Directed out	M	60.80	59.35	51.58	2.36
	SD	(18.29)	(15.41)	(16.43)	
Hostility Directed in	M	54.75	55.32	49.33	1.54
	SD	(16.62)	(14.91)	(12.22)	
Ambivalent Hostility	M	59.52	60.29	50.17	1.88
	SD	(22.16)	(22.43)	(21.27)	
Total Hostility	M	58.36	58.32	50.36	3.48*
	SD	(14.31)	(12.17)	(13.29)	
		(N = 30)	(N = 48)	(N = 45)	(2,122)
Self-Concept	M	49.68	51.75	53.97	1.90
	SD	(12.02)	(9.47)	(6.90)	

* $p < .05$; ** $p < .01$; *** $p < .001$

Table B.5. Partial Correlations Between Mothers' Responses to the Sexual Abuse and Pathology in the Child, Controlling for the Child's Age at the Time of Intake

			Mothers' Responses		
Pathology Scales	Protective Action (N = 144)	Punitive Action (N = 130)	Concern for Child (N = 156)	Concern for Self (N = 138)	Anger Toward Child (M = 136)
Louisville Total Severity Level (N = 112)	.04	.24**	-.01	-.01	.38***
Louisville Factors E-1 and E-2 (N = 88)					
Aggression	-.08	.38***	-.15	.04	.55***
Emotional Distress	.00	.23*	-.06	.06	.44***
Severe Symptoms	.01	.33**	.01	.16	.38***
School Problems	-.01	.23*	-.07	.11	.46***
Gottschalk (N = 88)					
Anxiety	-.01	.12	.05	.03	.16
Hostility Directed Outward	-.06	.06	-.01	-.00	-.09
Hostility Directed Inward	.05	.12	.02	.08	.02
Ambivalent Hostility	-.03	.01	.11	.10	.13
Total Hostility	-.03	.08	.06	.09	.04
Self-Concept (N = 123)	.06	-.08	-.09	-.10	-.19*

* $p < .05$; ** $p < .01$; *** $p < .001$

Table B.6. Analyses of Covariance:
Influence of Family Dissolution on Pathology

Pathology Scales		Status of Family			
		Family Remained Together	Child Removed	Parent Left	F (df)
Louisville Total Severity Level		(N = 63)	(N = 21)	(N = 27)	(2,110)
	M	42.82	48.97	41.98	3.42*
	SD	(8.62)	(13.81)	(8.05)	
Louisville Factors E-1 and E-2 (N = 88)		(N = 55)	(N = 15)	(N = 17)	(2,86)
Aggressive	M	57.86	72.77	58.15	5.63**
	SD	(12.75)	(25.46)	(13.33)	
Emotional Distress	M	54.24	60.82	52.82	2.60
	SD	(10.38)	(15.11)	(8.16)	
Serious Pathology	M	63.10	71.98	60.97	2.07
	SD	(14.63)	(24.74)	(13.21)	
School Problems	M	56.52	64.40	60.86	2.37
	SD	(10.63)	(20.30)	(11.41)	
Gottschalk (N = 88)		(N = 45)	(N = 21)	(N = 21)	(2,86)
Anxiety	M	47.08	49.04	48.73	<1
	SD				
Hostility Directed Outward	M	56.97	57.77	56.66	<1
	SD	(19.83)	(13.73)	(12.48)	
Hostility Directed Inward	M	54.72	51.99	51.94	
	SD	(15.19)	(11.47)	(15.87)	<1
Ambivalent Hostility	M	55.47	60.24	56.72	
	SD	(22.89)	(23.45)	(20.21)	<1
Total Hostility	M	55.72	56.67	55.11	
	SD	(14.23)	(12.59)	(12.88)	
Self-Concept (N = 123)		(N = 63)	(N = 29)	(N = 30)	
	M	53.20	50.26	50.99	<1
	SD	(9.46)	(9.42)	(9.17)	

* $p < .05$; ** $p < .01$; *** $p < .001$

APPENDIX C

Data Analyses for Chapter 6

Analyses of the relationships among variables describing mothers' reactions to the sexual abuse, their own personality problems, relationships with parents, and pervasive attitudes toward the child entailed two statistical techniques. When both measures involved continuous variables, Pearson Correlations measured the strength of association. When one variable was categorical (e.g., whether or not the mother had been sexually abused herself), analyses of variance were performed in which the mother's attitudes or responses to the sexual abuse were dependent variables and the categorical dimension was the independent variable.

Table C.1. Analyses of Variance: Influence of Offender's Relationship to Child on Mother's Reaction to the Abuse

		Natural Parent	Parent-Figure Not Blood Relative	Other Relative	Nonfamily	df	F
	(N)	28	30	32	48		
Protected	M	1.53	1.48	1.77	1.78	3,137	6.12***
Child	SD	.39	.41	.33	.35		
	(N)	22	27	30	45		
Punished	M	1.18	1.41	1.22	1.16	3,123	2.88*
Child	SD	.33	.42	.39	.33		
	(N)	30	32	35	51		
Concern	M	45.78	40.91	48.04	48.10	3,147	1.54
for Child[1]	SD	15.04	17.18	14.70	16.90		
	(N)	28	28	32	43		
Concern	M	50.43	52.61	49.81	50.09	3,130	<1
for Self[1]	SD	8.64	11.88	10.47	9.95		
	(N)	28	28	31	42		
Angry	M	1.11	1.86	1.32	1.21	3,128	6.93***
with Child	SD	.42	.97	.65	.61		

* $p < .05$; ** $p < .01$; *** $p < .001$
1. Scores have been converted to T-scores with a mean of 50 and standard deviation of 10.

Table C.2. Pearson Correlations: Mothers' Personality and Reactions to the Sexual Abuse

Mothers' Personality Dimensions	Reactions to the Sex Abuse				
	Protected Child	Punished Child	Concern for Child	Concern for Self	Anger toward Child
Submission	.08	.03	.00	.13	.14
Emotional Lability	.23*	−.02	.17	.29**	.28*
Social Withdrawal	.14	.07	.12	.18	.25*
Reality Distortion	−.02	−.01	.06	−.00	−.13
Negativism	.20	−.04	.16	.03	.04

* $p < .05$; ** $p < .01$; *** $p < .001$

Table C.3. Pearson Correlations: Mothers' Attitudes Toward Child
and Reactions to the Sexual Abuse

Mothers' Personality Dimensions	Reactions to Sex Abuse				
	Protected Child	Punished Child	Concern for Child	Concern for Self	Anger toward Child
Caring	.47***	-.46***	.59***	.25**	-.27**
Depending	-.21	.15	.09	.32**	.14
Burdened	-.30**	.45***	-.18*	.07	.49***
Hostile	-.27**	.30***	-.20*	.09	.67***

* $p < .05$; ** $p < .01$; *** $p < .001$

Table C.4. Pearson Correlations: Mothers' Relationships with Parents by
Mothers' Reactions to the Abuse and Attitudes Toward the Child

Mothers' Reactions to Abuse	Relationship with Mother	Relationship with Father
Protected child	-.10	-.30**
Punished child	-.17	-.01
Concern for child	-.23*	-.32**
Concern for self	-.03	.01
Anger toward child	-.03	-.03
Mothers' Attitudes Toward Child		
Caring	-.01	.06
Depending	-.28*	.07
Burdened	-.20	-.23*
Hostile	-.01	.06

* $p < .05$; ** $p < .01$; *** $p < .001$

Table C.5. Analyses of Variance: Relationship Between Mothers'
Reactions to the Sexual Abuse and Own History of Sexual Abuse

Reactions		Mother Never Abused	Mother Abused	df	F
Protected child	M	1.66	1.70	(1,105)	<1
	SD	.40	.33		
Punished child	M	1.19	1.23	(1,97)	<1
	SD	.36	.36		
Concern for child	M	3.02	3.21	(1,103)	1.86
	SD	.74	.62		
Concern for self	M	2.24	1.98	(1,103)	2.44
	SD	.86	.75		
Anger toward child	M	1.38	1.24	(1,103)	<1
	SD	.72	.62		

* $p < .05$; ** $p < .01$; *** $p < .001$

Table C.6. Analyses of Variance: Mothers' Attitudes Toward Child by
Relationship with Offender

Mothers' Attitudes Toward Child		Offender was				df	F
		Natural Father	Father-Figure	Other Relative	Nonfamily		
Caring	M	48.52	46.12[1]	49.48	52.70[1]	(3,111)	2.48*
	SD	10.09	10.86	10.79	8.17		
Depending	M	52.00	50.11	47.30	52.15	(3,77)	<1
	SD	13.18	8.44	7.99	10.94		
Burdened	M	47.59	52.52	50.14	49.32	(3,92)	<1
	SD	6.23	10.44	9.92	10.41		
Hostile	M	49.62	53.56[1]	51.92	46.88[1]	(3,110)	2.73*
	SD	9.47	12.30	10.78	7.90		

* $p < .05$; ** $p < .01$; *** $p < .001$
1. Designated with the same superscript differ from other at $p < .05$, Duncan's Multiple
Range Test.

Table C.7 Analyses of Variance: Influence of Type of Sex Act on Mothers' Reactions to the Abuse

Mothers' Reactions		Intercourse	Penetration	Fondling, Masturbation	Noncontact	df	F
	(N)	37	57	34	9		
Protected	M	1.65	1.65	1.68	1.75	3,136	<1
Child	SD	.38	.38	.40	.36		
	(N)	31	54	31	8		
Punished	M	1.21	1.23	1.19	1.12	3,123	<1
Child	SD	.38	.37	.36	.23		
	(N)	43	59	36	10		
Concern	M	44.46	48.15	43.32	49.48	3,147	<1
for Child[1]	SD	18.46	14.86	18.09	8.11		
	(N)	36	53	31	10		
Concern	M	51.19	51.34	49.52	49.60	3,129	<1
for Self[1]	SD	11.30	10.29	8.21	11.11		
	(N)	36	53	29	10		
Anger	M	1.31	1.34	1.41	1.40	3,127	<1
toward Child	SD	.75	.68	.73	.70		

* $p < .05$; ** $p < .01$; *** $p < .001$
1. Scores have been converted to T-scores with a mean of 50 and standard deviation of 10.

Table C.8. Analyses of Variance: Influence of Child's Sex on Mothers'
Reactions to the Abuse

		Female	Male	df	F
	(N)	115	29		
Protected	M	1.63	1.79	1,143	4.04**
Child	SD	.39	.33		
	(N)	101	29		
Punished	M	1.26	1.06	1,129	6.82***
Child	SD	.40	.18		
	(N)	122	34		
Concern	M	45.39	47.27	1,155	<1
for Child[1]	SD	16.15			
	(N)	108	30		
Concern	M	50.56	49.87	1,137	<1
for Self[1]	SD	10.39	9.35		
	(N)	107	29		
Anger	M	1.41	1.17	1,135	<1
toward Child	SD	.76	.53		

* $p < .05$; ** $p < .01$; *** $p < .001$
1. Scores have been converted to T-scores with a mean of 50 and standard deviation of 10.

Table C.9. Analyses of Variance: Influence of Child's Race on Mothers' Reactions to the Abuse

		White	Nonwhite	df	F
	(N)	111	33		
Protected	M	1.66	1.65	1,143	<1
Child	SD	.39	.37		
	(N)	101	29		
Punished	M	1.18	1.36	1,129	5.49*
Child	SD	.33	.46		
	(N)	117	39		
Concern	M	47.48	40.74	1,155	5.16*
for Child[1]	SD	14.37	20.29		
	(N)	109	29		
Concern	M	50.68	49.41	1,136	<1
for Self[1]	SD	10.10	10.39		
	(N)	108	28		
Anger	M	1.30	1.60	1,135	4.16*
Toward Child	SD	.66	.92		

* $p < .05$; ** $p < .01$; *** $p < .001$
1. Scores have been converted to T-scores with a mean of 50 and standard deviation of 10.

Table C.10. The Effect of the Length of Time Until the Child Revealed
the Sexual Abuse on Mothers' Reactions to the Abuse

		Immediately	Later	Never	df	F
	(N)	37	54	53		
Protected	M	1.83	1.58	1.63	2,143	5.16**
Child	SD	.29	.40	.40		
	(N)	35	51	44		
Punished	M	1.11	1.30	1.21	2,129	2.84
Child	SD	.27	.40	.38		
	(N)	37	59	60		
Concern	M	52.26	44.04	43.53	2,155	4.00*
for Child[1]	SD	8.95	17.41	17.66		
	(N)	37	51	50		
Concern	M	49.89	51.29	49.90	2,137	<1
for Self[1]	SD	9.92	10.76	9.78		
	(N)	36	51	49		
Angry	M	1.31	1.49	1.27	2,135	1.34
with Child	SD	.62	.83	.67		

* $p < .05$; ** $p < .01$; *** $p < .001$
1. Scores have been converted to T-scores with a mean of 50 and standard deviation of 10.

Table C.11. Mothers' History of Abuse and Relationship
with the Offender

Mother's Own Abuse	% abused for whom child's offender was:			
	Natural Parent	Parent Figure	Other Relative	Nonfamily
Sexual	55%	23%	35%	50%
Physical	17%	29%	55%	44%
Spouse	48%	39%	33%	35%

Table C.12. Analyses of Variance: Relationship of Mothers' Personality Problems and Relationship with Offender

Scales (N = 82)		Natural Parent (N = 20)	Parent-Figure (N = 16)	Other Relative (N = 18)	Nonfamily (N = 28)	E
			Offender was:			
Submission	M	65.45	65.79	66.56	59.25	1.19
	SD	17.04	16.12	15.35	13.21	
Emotional Lability	M	56.36	62.92	61.51	56.72	<1
	SD	18.99	22.48	16.38	17.33	
Social Withdrawal	M	62.92	59.16	59.97	55.62	<1
	SD	20.84	12.04	18.54	13.49	
Reality Distortion	M	53.98	45.83	56.99	57.84	1.43
	SD	20.00	18.66	23.97	15.83	
Negativism	M	39.98	40.58	54.99	47.51	1.95
	SD	18.34	23.49	24.59	20.35	

References

Abraham, K. (1907/1949). The experiencing of sexual traumas as a form of sexual activity (1907). *Selected Papers on Psychoanalysis, 1949,* 47-63.

Adams-Tucker, C. (1982). Proximate effects of sexual abuse in childhood: A report on 28 children. *American Journal of Psychiatry, 139,* 1252-1256.

Aguilera, D. C., & Messick, J. M. (1982). *Crisis intervention: Theory and methodology.* St. Louis, MO: C. V. Mosby.

Alexander, P. (1985). A system theory conceptualization of incest. *Family Process, 24,* 79-88.

Anderson, L. M., & Shafer, G. (1979). The character disordered family: A community treatment model for family sexual abuse. *American Journal of Orthopsychiatry, 49,* 436-445.

Anderson, S. C., Bach, C. M., & Griffin, S. (1981). *Psychosocial sequelae in intra-familial victims of sexual assault and abuse.* Paper presented at the Third International Congress on Child Abuse and Neglect, Amsterdam.

Badgley, R., Allard, H., McCormick, N., Proudfoot, P., Fortin, D., Ogilvie, D., Rae-Grant, Q., Gelinas, P., Pepin, L., & Sutherland, S. (1984). *Sexual offences against children* (vol. 1). Ottawa: Canadian Government Publishing Center.

Bagley, C., & Ramsey, R. (1986). Sexual abuse in childhood: Psychosocial outcomes and implications for social work practice. *Journal of Social Work and Human Sexuality, 4,* 33-47.

Bender, L., & Blau, A. (1937). The reaction of children to sexual relations with adults. *American Journal of Orthopsychiatry, 22,* 500-518.

Bender, L., & Grugett, A. (1952). A follow-up report on children who had atypical sexual experiences. *American Journal of Orthopsychiatry, 22,* 825-837.

Benward, J., & Densen-Gerber, J. (1973). Incest as a causative factor in antisocial behavior: An exploratory study. *Contemporary Drug Problems, 4,* 322-340.

Berliner, L., & Barbieri, M. K. (1984). The testimony of the child victim of sexual assault. *Journal of Social Issues, 40,* 125-137.

Boekelheide, P. D. (1978). Sexual adjustment in college women who experience incestuous relationships. *Journal of American College Health Association, 26,* 327-330.

Brant, R. S. T., & Herzog, J. M. (1979). *Psychiatric assessment of sexually abused toddlers.* Paper presented at the Meeting of the American Academy of Child Psychiatry, Houston, TX.

Briere, J., & Runtz, M. (1987). Post sexual abuse trauma: Data and implications for clinical practice. *Journal of Interpersonal Violence, 2,* 367-379.

Brooks, B. (1982). Familial influences in father-daughter incest. *Journal of Psychiatric Treatment and Evaluation, 4,* 117-124.

Browne, A., & Finkelhor, D. (1986). Impact of child sexual abuse: A review of the research. *Psychological Bulletin, 99,* 66-77.

Browning, D., & Boatman, B. (1977). Incest: Children at risk. *American Journal of Psychiatry, 134,* 69-72.

Brunold, H. J. (1964). Observations after sexual traumata suffered in childhood. *Excerpta Criminologica, 4,* 6-8.

Burgdorf, K. (1980). *Recognition and reporting of child maltreatment: Findings from the national study of the incidence and severity of child abuse and neglect.* Washington, DC: National Center on Child Abuse and Neglect.

Burgess, A. W. (1978). Divided loyalty in incest cases. In A. W. Burgess et al. (Eds.), *Sexual assault of children and adolescents.* Lexington, MA: Lexington Books.

Burgess, A. W., Groth, A. N., & Holmstrom L. L. (1974). *Rape: Victims of crisis.* Bowie, MD: Robert Brady.

Burgess, A. W., Groth, A. N., Holmstrom, L. L., & Sgroi, S. M. (Eds.). (1978). *Sexual assault of children and adolescents.* Lexington, MA: Lexington Books.

Burgess, A. W., & Holmstrom, L. L. (1975). Sexual trauma of children and adolescents: Pressure, sex and secrecy. *Nursing Clinics of North America, 10,* 551-563.

Burgess, A. W., Holmstrom, L. L., & McCausland, M. P. (1977). Child sexual assault by a family member: Decisions following disclosure. *Victimology: An International Journal, 2,* 236-250.

Burgess, A. W., Holmstrom, L. L., & McCausland, M. P. (1978). Counseling young victims and their families. In A. W. Burgess, A. N. Groth, L. L. Holmstrom, & S. M. Sgroi (Eds.), *Sexual assault of children and adolescents.* Lexington, MA: Lexington Books.

Burton, L. (1968). *Vulnerable children.* London: Routledge & Kegan Paul.

Caplan, G. (1964). *Principles of preventive psychiatry.* New York: Basic Books.

Connell, H. M. (1978). Incest—A family problem. *Medical Journal of Australia, 2,* 362-367.

Conte, J. (1982). Sexual abuse of children: Enduring issues for social work. In J. Conte & D. Shore (Eds.), *Social work and sexual abuse* (pp. 1-20). New York: Haworth.

Conte, J. R., & Berliner, L. (1987). The impact of child sexual abuse on children: Empirical findings. In L. Walker (Ed.), *Handbook on sexual abuse of children: Assessment and treatment issues.* New York: Springer.

Conte, J. R., & Schuerman, J. R. (1987). Factors associated with an increased impact of child sexual abuse. *Child Abuse and Neglect, 11,* 201-211.

Cormier, B. M., Kennedy, M., & Sangowicz, J. (1962). Psychodynamics of father-daughter incest. *Canadian Psychiatric Association Journal, 7*, 203-216.

Corwin, D. L., Berliner, L., Goodman, G., Goodwin, J., & White, S. (1987). Child sexual abuse and custody disputes: No easy answers. *Journal of Interpersonal Violence, 2*, 91.

Cupoli, J. M., & Sewell, P. M. (1988). One thousand fifty-nine children with a chief complaint of sexual abuse. *Child Abuse and Neglect, 12*, 151-162.

DeFrancis, V. (1969). *Protecting the child victim of sex crimes committed by adults.* Denver, CO: American Humane Association.

DeFrancis, V. (1971). Protecting the child victim of sex crimes committed by adults. *Federal Probation, 35*, 15-20.

DeVine, R. A. (1980). The sexually abused child in the emergency room. In B. M. Jones, L. L. Jenstrom, & K. MacFarlane (Eds.), *Sexual abuse of children: Selected readings.* DHHS Publication No. OHDS 78-30161. Washington, DC: Government Printing Office.

Dietz, C. A., & Craft, J. L. (1980). Family dynamics of incest: A new perspective. *Social Casework: The Journal of Contemporary Social Work, 61*, 602-609.

Eist, H. I., & Mandel, A. U. (1968). Family treatment of ongoing incest behavior. *Family Process, 7*, 216-232.

Everson, M. D., & Boat, B. W. (1989). False allegations of sexual abuse by children and adolescents. *Journal of the American Academy of Child and Adolescent Psychiatry, 28*, 230-235.

Faller, K. C. (1988). The myth of the "collusive mother." *Journal of Interpersonal Violence, 3*, 190-195.

Fields, S. M. (1981). Parent-child relationships, childhood sexual abuse and adult interpersonal behavior in female prostitutes. *Dissertation Abstracts International, 42*, 2053B.

Finkelhor, D. (1979). *Sexually victimized children.* New York: Free Press.

Finkelhor, D. (1983). Removing the child—Prosecuting the offender in cases of child sexual abuse: Evidence from the National Reporting System for Child Abuse and Neglect. *Child Abuse and Neglect, 7*, 195-205.

Finkelhor, D. (1984). *Child sexual abuse: New theory and research.* New York: Free Press.

Finkelhor, D. (1986). *A sourcebook on child sexual abuse.* Beverly Hills, CA: Sage.

Finkelhor, D. (1987). The trauma of child sexual abuse: Two models. *Journal of Interpersonal Violence, 2*, 348-366.

Finkelhor, D., & Hotaling, G. T. (1984). Sexual abuse in the national incidence study of child abuse and neglect: An appraisal. *Child Abuse and Neglect, 8*, 23-33.

Finkelhor, D., Gomes-Schwartz B., & Horowitz, J. (1984). Professionals' responses. In D. Finkelhor, *Child sexual abuse: New theory and research,* pp. 200-220. New York: Free Press.

Forward, S., & Buck, C. (1978). *Betrayal of innocence: Incest and its devastation,* p. 45. New York: Penguin.

Fox, R. (1980). *The red lamp of incest.* New York: E. P. Dutton.

Fraiberg, S., Adelson E., & Shapiro V. (1975). Ghosts in the nursery: A psychoanalytic approach to the problems of impaired infant-mother relationships. *Journal of the American Academy of Child Psychiatry, 14*, 387-421.

Friedrich, W. N. (1986). Behavior problems in sexually abused young children. *Journal of Pediatric Psychology, 11*, 47-57.

Friedrich, W. N., Beilke, R. L., & Urquiza, A. J. (1987). Children from sexually abusive families: A behavioral comparison. *Journal of Interpersonal Violence, 2*, 391-402.

Freud, S. (1953). *A general introduction to psychoanalysis.* New York: Pulmer.

Fromuth, M. E. (1986). The relationship of childhood sexual abuse with later psychological and sexual adjustment in a sample of college women. *Child Abuse and Neglect, 10*, 5-15.

Funk, J. B. (1980). Management of sexual molestation in preschoolers. *Clinical Pediatrics, 19*, 686-688.

Gagnon, J. (1965). Female child victims of sex offenses. *Social Problems, 13*, 176-192.

Gebhard, P. H., Gagnon, J. H., Pomeroy, W. P., & Christenson, C. V. (1965). *Sex offenders: An analysis of types.* New York: Harper & Row.

Gelles, R. J. (1973). Child abuse as psychopathology: A sociological critique and reformulation. *American Journal of Orthopsychiatry, 43*, 611-621.

Giaretto, H. (1976). Humanistic treatment of father-daughter incest. In R. E. Helfer & C. H. Kempe (Eds.), *Child abuse and neglect—The family and the community.* Cambridge, MA: Ballinger.

Giaretto, H. (1981). A comprehensive child sexual abuse treatment program. In P. B. Mrazek & C. H. Kempe (Eds.), *Sexually abused children and their families.* Oxford, England: Pergamon Press.

Goldstein, J., Freud, A., & Solnit, A. J. (1979). *Before the best interests of the child.* New York: Free Press.

Gomes-Schwartz, B., Horowitz, J. M., & Sauzier, M. (1985). Severity of emotional distress among sexually abused preschool, school-age and adolescent children. *Hospital and Community Psychiatry, 35*, 503-508.

Goodwin, J., McCarthy, T., & DiVasto, P. (1981). Prior incest in mothers of abused children. *Child Abuse and Neglect, 5*, 87-96.

Gottschalk, L. A., Uliana, R. L., & Holgard, J. C. (1979). Preliminary validation of a set of content analysis scales applicable to verbal samples for measuring the magnitude of psychological states in children. *Psychiatry Research, 1*, 71-82.

Green, A. H. (1986). True and false allegations of sexual abuse in child custody disputes. *Journal of the American Academy of Child Psychiatry, 25*, 449-456.

Groth, A. N. (1978). Guidelines for the assessment and management of the offender. In A. W. Burgess, A. N. Groth, L. L. Holmstrom, & S. M. Sgroi (Eds.), *Sexual assault of children and adolescents.* Lexington, MA: Lexington.

Groth, A. N. (1979). *Men who rape: The psychology of the offender.* New York: Plenum Press.

Groth, A. N., & Birnbaum, H. J. (1978). Adult sexual orientation and attraction to underage persons. *Archives of Sexual Behavior, 7*, 175-181.

Groth, A. N., Burgess, A. W., Birnbaum, J. J., & Gary, T. S. (1978). A study of the child molester: Myths and realities. *LAE Journal of the American Criminal Justice Association, 41*, No. 1, Winter/Spring.

Groth, A. N., Burgess, A. W., & Holmstrom, L. L. (1977). Rape: Power, anger and sexuality. *American Journal of Psychiatry, 134*, 1239-1243.

Gruber, K., & Jones, R. (1983). Identifying determinants of risk of sexual victimization of youth. *Child Abuse and Neglect, 7*, 17-24.

Henderson, D. J. (1972). Incest: A synthesis of data. *Canadian Psychiatric Association Journal, 17,* 299-313.

Herman, J. (1981). Father-daughter incest. *Professional Psychology, 12,* 76-80.

Herman, J. (1982). *Father-daughter incest.* Cambridge, MA: Harvard University Press.

Herman, J., & Hirschman, L. (1977). Father-daughter incest. *Signs: Journal of Women in Culture and Society , 2,* 735-756.

Herman, J., & Hirschman, L. (1981). Families at risk for father-daughter incest. *American Journal of Psychiatry, 138,* 967-970.

James, J., & Meyerding, J. (1977). Early sexual experience and prostitution. *American Journal of Psychiatry, 134,* 1381-1385.

James, K. L. (1977). Incest: The teenager's perspective. *Psychotherapy: Theory, Research, and Practice, 14,* 146-155.

Justice, B., & Justice, R. (1979). *The broken taboo: Sex in the family.* New York: Human Sciences Press.

Kaufman, I., Peck, A., & Tagiuri, C. K. (1954). The family constellation and overt incestuous relations between father and daughter. *American Journal of Orthopsychiatry, 24,* 266-279.

Kempe, C. H. (1978). Sexual abuse, another hidden pediatric problem. *Pediatrics, 62,* 382-389.

Kiser, L. J., Ackerman, B. J., Brown, E., Edwards, N. B., McColgan, E., Pugh, R., & Pruitt, D. B. (1988). Post-traumatic stress disorder in young children: A reaction to purported sexual abuse. *Journal of the American Academy of Child and Adolescent Psychiatry, 27,* 645-649.

Kroth, J. A. (1979). *Child sexual abuse.* Springfield, IL: Charles C Thomas.

Kubler-Ross, E. (1969). *On death and dying.* New York: MacMillan.

Landis, J. (1956). Experiences of 500 children with adult sexual deviants. *Psychiatric Quarterly Supplement, 30,* 91-109.

Lewis, M., & Sarrel, P. M. (1969). Some psychological aspects of seduction, incest, and rape in childhood. *Journal of the American Academy of Child Psychiatry, 8,* 606-619.

Lindholm, K. (1984). *Trends in child sexual abuse: A study of 611 reported cases in Los Angeles County.* Paper presented at the 64th Annual Convention of the Western Psychological Association, Los Angeles.

Lloyd, R. (1976). *For money or love: Boy prostitution in America.* New York: Vanguard.

Lukianowicz, N. (1972). Incest. In Paternal incest, II: Other types of incest. *British Journal of Psychiatry, 120,* 301-313.

Lustig, N., Dresser, J. W., Spellman, S. W., & Murray, T. B. (1966). Incest: A family group survival pattern. *Archives of General Psychiatry, 14,* 31-40.

Lynch, M. (1985). Child abuse before Kempe: An historical literature review. *Child Abuse and Neglect, 9,* 7-15.

MacFarlane, K. (1978). Sexual abuse of children. In J. R. Chapman & M. Gaters (Eds.), *The victimization of women.* Beverly Hills, CA: Sage.

Machotka, P., Pittman, P. S., & Flomenhaft, K. (1967). Incest as a family affair. *Family Process, 6,* 98-116.

MacVicar, K. (1979). Psychotherapeutic issues in the treatment of sexually abused girls. *Journal of the American Academy of Child Psychiatry, 19,* 342-353.

Maisch, H. (1972). *Incest* (C. Bearne Trans.). New York: Stein & Day.

Martinson, F. M. (1973). *Infant and child sexuality: A sociological perspective.* St. Peter, MN: The Book Mark.

McLeer, S. V., Beblinger, E., Atkins, M. S., Foa, E. B., & Ralphe, D. L. (1988). Post-traumatic stress disorder in sexually abused children. *Journal of the American Academy of Child and Adolescent Psychiatry, 27,* 650-654.

McIntyre, K. (1981). Role of mothers in father-daughter incest: A feminist analysis. *Social Work, 26,* 462-466.

Meiselman, K. C. (1978). *Incest: A psychological study of causes and effects with treatment recommendations.* San Francisco: Jossey-Bass.

Mian, M., Wehrspann, W., Klajner-Diamond, H., LeBaron, D., & Winder, C. (1986). Review of 125 children 6 years of age and under who were sexually abused. *Child Abuse and Neglect, 10,* 223-229.

Miller, L. C. (1981). *Louisville behavior checklist.* Los Angeles: Western Psychological Services.

Murphy, S. M., Kilpatrick, D. G., Amick-McMullan, A., Vernonen, L. J., Paduhovich, J., Best, C. L., Villeponteaux, L. A., & Saunders, B. E. (1988). Current psychological functioning of child sexual assault survivors: A community study. *Journal of Interpersonal Violence, 3,* 55-79.

Nakashima, I. T., & Zakus, G. E. (1977). Incest: Review and clinical experience. *Pediatrics, 60,* 696-701.

National Center for Child Abuse and Neglect (1978). *Child sexual abuse: Incest, assault and sexual exploitation.* Washington, DC: Department of Health, Education, and Welfare.

National Center for Child Abuse and Neglect (1981). *National incidence study of child abuse and neglect.* Washington, DC: Department of Health and Human Services.

Newman, M. B., & San Martino, M. R. (1971). The child and the seriously disturbed parent. *Journal of the American Academy of Child Psychiatry, 10,* 358-374.

Peters, J. J. (1976). Children who were victims of sexual assault and the psychology of offenders. *American Journal of Psychotherapy, 30,* 398-421.

Peters, S. D. (1984). *The relationship between childhood sexual victimization and adult depression among Afro-American and white women.* Unpublished doctoral dissertation, University of California at Los Angeles (University Microfilms No. 84-28, 555).

Pfohl, S. J. (1977). The "discovery" of child abuse. *Social Problems, 24,* 310-323.

Phelan, P. (1986). The process of incest: Biologic father and stepfather families. *Child Abuse and Neglect, 10,* 531-539.

Pierce, R., & Pierce, L. H. (1985). The sexually abused child: A comparison of male and female victims. *Child Abuse and Neglect, 9,* 191-199.

Pittman, F. S. (1977). Incest. *Current Psychiatric Therapies, 17,* 129-134.

Rascovsky, A., & Rascovsky, M. (1950). On consummated incest. *International Journal of Psychoanalysis, 31,* 42.

Reinhart, M. A. (1987). Sexually abused boys. *Child Abuse and Neglect, 11,* 229-235.

Renvoize, J. (1982). *Incest: A family pattern.* London: Routledge & Kegan Paul.

Riemer, S. A. (1940). A research note on incest. *American Journal of Sociology, 45,* 566-575.

Righton, P. (1981). The adult. In B. Taylor (Ed.), *Perspectives on paedophilia.* London: Batsford.

Risin, L. I., & Koss, M. P. (1987). The sexual abuse of boys: Prevalence and descriptive characteristics of childhood victimizations. *Journal of Interpersonal Violence, 2,* 309-323.

Rosenfeld, A. A. (1979). Endogamic incest and victim-perpetrator model. *American Journal of Diseases of Children, 133,* 406-410.

Roth, R. A. (1978). *Child sexual abuse: Incest, assault, and sexual exploitation.* A special report from the National Center on Child Abuse and Neglect. Department of Health, Education and Welfare. (DHEW Publication No. OHDS 79-30166). Washington, DC: Government Printing Office.

Russell, D.E.H. (1983). The incidence and prevalence of intrafamilial and extrafamilial sexual abuse of female children. *Child Abuse and Neglect, 7,* 133-146.

Russell, D.E.H. (1984). The prevalence and seriousness of incestuous abuse: Stepfathers vs. biological fathers. *Child Abuse and Neglect, 8,* 15-22.

Russell, D.E.H. (1986). *The secret trauma: Incest in the lives of girls and women.* New York: Basic Books.

Russell, D.E.H., Schurman, R. A., & Trocki, K. (1988). The long-term effects of incestuous abuse: A comparison of Afro-American and white American victims. In G. E. Wyatt & G. J. Powell (Eds.), *Lasting effects of child sexual abuse* (pp. 119-134). Newbury Park, CA: Sage.

Sarles, R. M. (1975). Incest. *Pediatric Clinics of North America, 22,* 633-642.

Sgroi, S. M. (1982). *Handbook of clinical intervention in child sexual abuse.* Lexington, MA: Lexington.

Silbert, M. H., & Pines, A. M. (1981). Sexual abuse as an antecedent to prostitution. *Child Abuse and Neglect, 5,* 407-411.

Simrel, K., Berg, R., & Thomas, J. (1979). Crisis management of sexually abused children. *Pediatric Annals, 8,* 317-325.

Sirles, E. A., Smith, J. A., & Kusama, H. (1989). Psychiatric status of intrafamilial child sexual abuse victims. *Journal of the American Academy of Child and Adolescent Psychiatry, 28,* 225-229.

Summit, R., & Kryso, J. (1978). Sexual abuse of children: A clinical spectrum. *American Journal of Orthopsychiatry, 48,* 237-251.

Swanson, D. W. (1968). Adult sexual abuse of children. *Diseases of the Nervous System, 29,* 677-683.

Tilelli, J. A., Turek, D., & Jaffe, A. C. (1980). Sexual abuse of children. *New England Journal of Medicine, 302,* 319-349.

Tormes, Y. M. (1968/1972). *Child victims of incest.* Denver, CO: The American Humane Association, Children's Division.

Trainor, C. (1984). *Sexual maltreatment in the United States: A five-year perspective.* Paper presented at the International Congress on Child Abuse and Neglect, Montreal.

Tsai, M., Feldman-Summers, S., & Edgar, M. (1979). Childhood molestation variables related to differential impacts on psychosocial functioning on adult women. *Journal of Abnormal Psychology, 88,* 407-417.

Tsai, M., & Wagner, N. (1978). Therapy groups for women sexually molested as children. *Archives of Sexual Behavior, 7,* 417-429.

Vander Mey, B. J. (1988). The sexual victimization of male children: A review of previous research. *Child Abuse and Neglect, 12,* 61-72.

Virkkunen, M. (1975). Victim-precipitated pedophilia offences. *British Journal of Criminology, 15,* 175-180.

von Kraft-Ebing, R. (1935). *Psychopathia sexualis*. New York: Physicians and Surgeons Book Co.

Ward, E. (1985). *Father-daughter incest*. New York: Grove.

Weinberg, K. (1955). *Incest behavior*. New Jersey: The Citadel Press.

Weiner, I. B. (1962). Father-daughter incest: A clinical report. *Psychiatric Quarterly, 36*, 607-632.

Weiss, E. H., & Berg, R. F. (1982). Child victims of sexual assault: Impact of court procedures. *Journal of the American Academy of Child Psychiatry, 21*, 513-518.

Weiss, J., Rogers, E., Darwin, M., & Dutton, C. (1955). A study of girl sex victims. *Psychiatric Quarterly, 29*, 1-27.

Whitcomb, D. (1986). *Prosecuting child sexual abuse—New approaches*. NIJ Reports/SNI 197, National Institute of Justice, U.S. Department of Justice, 2-6.

Wyatt, G. E. (1985). The sexual abuse of Afro-American and White American women in childhood. *Child Abuse and Neglect, 9*, 507-519.

Wyatt, G. E., & Peters, S. D. (1986a). Issues in the definition of child sexual abuse in prevalence research. *Child Abuse and Neglect, 10*, 231-240.

Wyatt, G. E., & Peters, S. D. (1986b). Methodological considerations in research on the prevalence of child sexual abuse. *Child Abuse and Neglect, 10*, 241-251.

Yorukoglu, A., & Kemph, J. (1969). Children not severely damaged by incest with a parent. *Journal of the Academy of Child Psychiatry, 8*, 111-124

Zetzel, E. R., & Meissner, W. W. (1973). *Basic concepts of psychoanalytic psychiatry*. New York: Basic Books.

Index

About the Authors

ALBERT P. CARDARELLI is Senior Associate at the John W. McCormack Insitute of Public Affairs and Lecturer in Sociology at the University of Massachusetts at Boston. He has a Ph.D in sociology from the University of Pennsylvania and a J.D. degree from Suffolk University Law School. He is a former Professor and Co-Director of the Sociology Department at Boston University. He has published extensively in the areas of delinquency prevention, prisoners' legal rights, and child sexual abuse. At present his research interests include legal theory, research on unsolved homicides, and mental retardation and the law. He has served as an advisor to the Office of Juvenile Justice and Delinquency Prevention, the National Council of Crime and Delinquency, along with various national, state, and local agencies involved in criminal justice. He is a member of the American Academy of Criminal Justice Sciences, the American Society of Criminology, and the National Humanities Faculty.

BEVERLY GOMES-SCHWARTZ was Research Director of the Family Crisis Program at New England Medical Center, and Assistant Professor, Department of Psychiatry, Tufts University Medical School at the time the research for the present book was conducted. She had previously been an instructor at Harvard Medical School/McLean Hospital. In addition to several journal articles and chapters on child sexual abuse, Dr. Gomes-Schwartz has published in the area of psychotherapy outcome. She holds an MA and Ph.D. in psychology from Vanderbilt University. Since the completion of the research for this volume, she obtained an MBA degree from Babson College. She is now a manager in Information Services for Fidelty Investments, Boston.

JONATHAN HOROWITZ (M.D.) is a graduate of Cornell University, Tufts University School of Medicine, and the Boston Psychoanalytic Institute. He is certified by the American Board of Psychiatry and Neurology with special certification in child psychiatry. Formerly he was Director of the child guidance clinic at New England Medical Center in Boston, and is now Chief of Psychiatry at Carney Hospital in Boston and maintains a private psychiatric practice in Waban, MA. He served as project director and clinical director for the study "Sexually Exploited Children: Service and Research Program," funded by the office of Juvenile Justice and Delinquency Prevention. His work in the field of child sexual abuse has included teaching courses for mental health clinicians, numerous presentations at professional meetings, and co-authoring several publications. He is also Assistant Clinical Professor of Psychiatry at Boston University School of Medicine.

NOTES

NOTES

NOTES

Please remember that this is a library book,
and that it belongs only temporarily to each
person who uses it. Be considerate. Do
not write in this, or any, library book.